Aquinas's Neoplatonism in the
Summa Theologiae on God

Aquinas's Neoplatonism in the *Summa Theologiae* on God

Wayne J. Hankey

ST. AUGUSTINE'S PRESS
South Bend, Indiana

Library of Congress Cataloging in Publication Data

Names: Hankey, W. J., author.
Title: Aquinas's neoplatonism in the Summa theologiae on God : a short introduction / by Wayne J. Hankey ; foreword by Matthew D. Walz.
Description: 1st [edition]. | South Bend, Indiana : St. Augustines Press,
2016. | Includes bibliographical references.
Identifiers: LCCN 2016012549 | ISBN 9781587310201 (clothbound : alk. paper)
Subjects: LCSH: Thomas, Aquinas, Saint, 1225?-1274. Summa theologica. | God
(Christianity)--History of doctrines--Middle Ages, 600-1500.
Trinity--History of doctrines--Middle Ages, 600-1500. Neoplatonism.
Classification: LCC BX1749.T6 H36 2016 | DDC 231--dc23 LC record available at
http://lccn.loc.gov/2016012549

TABLE OF CONTENTS

Foreword

Thomas Aquinas thinks and teaches sapientially; he thinks and teaches, that is, from and toward wisdom. A prudent steward of the tradition, he draws from its treasury things both old and new, putting them in such an order (as befits the *sapiens*) as to enable those who study his works to grow in truth—which is, Aquinas maintains, the ultimate end of the universe. In the following short but dense book, as he did in the 2015 Aquinas Lecture at the University of Dallas, Professor Wayne J. Hankey highlights Thomas's sapiential thinking and teaching, especially in the highly metaphysical treatment of God in the First Part of the *Summa theologiae*. Through deep familiarity with Thomas's works and sources as well as with the scholarship of the last century, Professor Hankey shows how Thomas draws discernfully from the Neoplatonic tradition in giving an account of God and creation, and how Thomas gives that account according to a recognizably Neoplatonic order whereby one winds up, as it were, right where one began—though enriched, of course, with greater insight and deeper love of our creative Source and beatifying End.

During his lecture, Professor Hankey briefly compared the *Summa theologiae* to the cathedrals of Europe constructed during the Middle Ages. As Professor Hankey himself noted, this is not a novel comparison, although it is one worth returning to; for it provides an imaginative basis for considering the "craftsmanship" that entered into Thomas's "construction" of the *Summa theologiae*. Those medieval cathedrals are huge, cavernous, awe-inspiring; their architects dreamed large. At the same time those cathedrals evidence effective engineering, meticulous workmanship, and attentive artistry, all the way down to the tiniest of details. The *Summa theologiae* bears the same features. Its task is grand—indeed, no less than to lead us to share as much as we can *in via* in the vision of the blessed. Yet the work manifests Thomas's scrupulous attention to every distinction, term, and logical move. Moreover, as Professor Hankey hints at it in this book, it is not unfitting to identify Thomas's construction of the *Summa theologiae* as fundamentally religious in character, insofar as it involved acts of *devotio* and *oratio* whereby Thomas elevates his own will and intellect (and ours as well) in just measure toward an immeasurable God. Indeed, to see the *Summa theologiae* in a religious light like this not only enhances the comparison of it to those cathedrals in which the God-man is made sacramentally present, but also aligns Thomas's thinking with numerous Neoplatonists who regarded their philosophical endeavors to be essentially religious in character, inasmuch as their contemplation of reality was meant to be dispositive toward theurgical action.

Professor Hankey notes in his preface that he has been consoled "to have spent so much time in theological contemplation through Thomas's inexhaustible text." It is evident from his scholarly work, though, that Professor Hankey appreciates not only the truth of

Thomas's contemplation of God delineated in the *Summa theologiae*, but also its beauty. It is beautiful to behold, Professor Hankey shows, how Thomas harmonizes so many major voices in the tradition. As the first few chapters of this book evidence, the Neoplatonists are clearly among those voices, providing more of an undertone for Thomas's thinking than is usually acknowledged. We should be grateful to Professor Hankey for having the ears to hear the Neoplatonic reverberations in Thomas's writings, a perceptivity he has achieved owing to countless hours of historical, philosophical, and theological research. Professor Hankey's willingness to share his erudition regarding Thomas's works helps us to value even more the inimitable synthesizing mind of the *Doctor communis*.

It is also beautiful to behold, Professor Hankey shows, just how masterfully Thomas crafts the *Summa theologiae* according to embedded encirclings of thought. Professor Hankey brings to light a fractal-like structure in the *Summa theologiae*, that is, smaller circles of thought enveloped by larger ones, which in turn are enveloped by even larger ones. These encirclings may be likened to those ripples of concentric waves that swell outward when one tosses a small stone into a large pond. The stone tossed into the depths of Thomas's mind was not so small, however; it was no less than the great "I am who am" spoken by the person of God to Moses after Moses had beheld that wondrous sign on Sinai, a bush burning but not consumed. God as *ipsum esse per se subsistens*, existence itself subsisting in its own right, the most really real reality there can be—this was the great metaphysical stone tossed into Thomas's mind, and in the second half of this book Professor Hankey maps out the rippling waves that flow outward from it into the whole of the *Summa theologiae*.

Now, when we draw a circle, what do we do? We pick some point of origin, proceed curvingly away from it, and then make our way back to the original point. There is something captivatingly simple about a circle and the motion that brings it about. This struck me recently when I was watching two of my daughters as they spun a top on our living room table. Once they got the hang of it, they were able to watch the top spin for upwards of a minute. During these successful spins, they were transfixed, as was I; a well-spun top can be transfixing. We beheld in childlike amazement the top's active persistence in its speedy, spinning stability, and meanwhile we lost track of time and our surroundings. A top captivates us by its dynamic restfulness, its seemingly motionless motion, which hints that somehow its circular motion is able to harness the infinite. A circle brings that which is end-less into a manageable intelligibility, albeit one that escapes full rational articulation. Indeed, formulas describing circles introduce that strange number, *pi*—a number symbolized by a Greek letter—which reminds us that calculating reason is inadequate to the full truth of a circle.

I don't know if Thomas ever played with tops as a young boy. I do know, however, thanks in large part to Professor Hankey's scholarly work, that Thomas was indebted to the Neoplatonists, who preserved in their works the spirit of the original Greek philosophers, an aspect of which was a love of circles. Indeed, in various ways circularity informs the Greek philosophical understanding of reality.

Recall Parmenides' desire to learn "the un-shaken heart of well-rounded truth"; or Plato's inward-bending theory of recollection, imaged in the Phaedrus by a circular journey around the heavens; or Aristotle's Prime Mover, "Thought Thinking Thought," giving rise through self-reflexive activity to the circular motions that govern the physical cosmos. Such examples highlighting circularity abound among Greek thinkers, including Euclid's beautiful geometrical construction at the outset of the *Elements*, where the coupling of two circles begets an equilateral triangle—thereby suggesting that circularity, so mysterious in its simplicity, so hard to pin down rationally, nonetheless underlies the rectilinear figures whose intelligibility we have an easier time articulating with exactness.

As Professor Hankey presents the *Summa theologiae*, Thomas too sees that the circular often underlies the rational. Thomas sees, one might say, that in order to think straight, one may have to think circularly. This is true even—or, perhaps, especially—when attending to the highest reality that one can think, namely, God himself as pure existence. Thus, as Professor Hankey points out, Thomas's account of God progresses circularly according to a dynamic of remaining–going-out–returning. In particular, Professor Hankey emphasizes the circle of Trinitarian life, because this circular communion of Persons stands at the beginning and end of reality and, therefore, at the beginning and end of our apprehending the truth of reality: the Father, eternally giving existence; the Son, eternally accepting existence from the Father; the Spirit, eternally connecting Father and Son as the ecstatic reciprocal love between them.

But isn't circular motion pointless? Doesn't one simply end up where one began? In fact, logically speaking, we often refer to "vicious circles," those self-defeating lines of argument in which one presumes precisely what one is trying to prove. Professor Hankey makes it clear, though, how Thomas progresses in his account of God in the *Summa theologiae*. Thomas's encirclings, in other words, are not of a logically vicious sort; they are, rather, of a methodologically virtuous sort. They map out a contemplatively fruitful *methodos*, a profitable way of traveling along a path. And when it comes to understanding reality in an ultimate sense, the path begins, goes forth, and ends in God's pure *esse*, and along the way progress is made insofar as the pure existence of God is made more real to us and, little by little, more thinkable and speakable by us. Hence, as we move through the First Part of the *Summa theologiae*, we begin to appropriate in a human way the full ramifications of the great "I am who am" who is also Trinity.

It may be helpful to think of Thomas's circular *methodos* in the *Summa theologiae* as something like simply going for a walk. My wife and I like to go for walks whenever we find the time to get away. Sometimes when we do so one of our young daughters stands at the front door and asks, "Where are you going?" "We're going for a walk," I usually respond, which inexplicably settles the question. Would a truer answer be: "We're going home, right where we're starting from"? For that is "where" we go: beginning from home, we circle around the neighborhood and end up just where we began. What a waste of time! Yet this seemingly non-progressive progression from home to home provides a context within which my wife and I truly do progress, deliberating about this or that child of ours, figuring out plans for the weekend, or (most preferably) simply getting to know each other better. Moreover, to return to the religious character of the *Summa theologiae*, there is something ritualistic about these walks, as there is, I think, in Thomas's work. The regularity, predictability, and enclosing finiteness of both a walk and the circular *methodos* of the *Summa theologiae* provide a framework for mindful attentiveness. The ritualistic character of the walks I take with my wife allows us to focus on one another and on whatever issues require our deliberation. And it is my experience that the ritualistic character of the *Summa theologiae*, in an almost liturgical manner, allows one to focus on reality in a manner that enables reason to achieve those penetrating insights into reality and God of which, girded by faith, it is truly capable.

In the First Part of the *Summa theologiae*, then, by thinking in, through, and around God as pure existence, Thomas gradually

hones in on the center of the truth of all reality. As Professor Hankey shows, Thomas
slowly unfolds the truth about God in a ped-
agogically appropriate manner: a simple God,
who is pure existence, is also good and one.
This one God both knows and loves himself.
And this one, self-knowing, self-loving God is
three Persons, Father, Son, and Spirit, who in
turn lovingly and freely chooses to create.
With each circular turn, Thomas unveils a little more the inexhaustible truth of a God who
identified himself as "I am who am." And it
turns out, wonder of wonders, that *ipsum esse
per se subsistens* is Trinity, giving–accepting–
connecting. *Esse* in its purity is a circle of Persons containing inwardly all the perfections of
each and every creature to which it outwardly
gives existence. It is this wonder to which Professor Hankey draws our attention in this
book, and he shows that by understanding the
Neoplatonic influence on Thomas's thinking,
we are more apt to recognize the artistry of
Thomas's thoroughgoing account of God and
creation in the *Summa theologiae*.

"From Impassibility to Self-Affectivity:
The Trinitarian Metaphysics of *Esse* in St.

Thomas's *Summa theologiae*": this was the title of the lecture Professor Hankey delivered at the University of Dallas, and it is the title of chapter four of this book. According to Thomas, as pure existence, God is "impassible." Pure existence is pure act, the act of all acts, and thus is not capable of being changed or modified by something. As pure *esse*, God has no "passive potency"; hence, properly speaking, God is not open to receiving anything from some other reality. Indeed, as Thomas sometimes says—thinking along Neoplatonic lines, as Professor Hankey points out—God's uniqueness as a reality consists precisely in his pure goodness, which entails that divine *esse* is of such a sort that nothing can be added to it. The full perfection and completeness of existence already belongs to God, and an aspect of that perfection and completeness is what Professor Hankey calls "self-affectivity," an internal relationality within God that we begin to grasp, at least a little bit, when we hold firmly that the Father is eternally giving existence to the Son while the Son is eternally accepting existence from the Father. At the very heart of all existence, in the perfect and complete existence that God is, there is eternal giving to and accepting from another. The Father generously gives; the Son graciously accepts; and between them arises the ecstatic, unifying love that is the Spirit. What Professor Hankey's reading of the *Summa theologiae* brings out, then, is that joy-filled generosity and hospitality are etched into *esse* itself in its most complete, uncreated occurrence. Importantly, then, we ourselves obtain a share in this completeness of existence not merely by existing, but also by thoughtfully willing to exist in relation to others in a manner marked by joy-filled generosity and hospitality. In fact, much of the *Summa theologiae* after the First Part may be seen as trying to describe this manner of truly virtuous human living (Second Part), which is made possible for us by the paradigmatic generosity of the Word-becoming-flesh and the hospitality of his Church, offering sacraments for us who require such remedies (Third Part).

Such is the vision of the *Summa theologiae* to which Professor Hankey's interpretive insights in this book can give rise. By calling attention to the Neoplatonic influences on

Thomas's thinking, Professor Hankey allows us to experience in our reading of the *Summa theologiae* that feature of reality so dear to the heart of a Neoplatonist, namely, beauty. For opening our eyes to this aspect of Thomas's thought, especially in the *Summa theologiae*, I am grateful to Professor Hankey, as I hope you too will be upon completing this book. It is also my hope that Professor Hankey will continue to share his work as a scholar, philosopher, and theologian with us for many years to come, thereby opening our eyes even more widely to the beauty of existence encountered through the seemingly inexhaustible texts of Thomas Aquinas.

Matthew D. Walz
Philosophy Department
University of Dallas

Preface

On the Feast of St. Thomas Aquinas, 2015, I had the privilege of delivering the Aquinas Lecture at the University of Dallas. Entitled "From Impassibility to Self-Affectivity: the Trinitarian Metaphysics of *Esse* in Thomas's *Summa Theologiae*," it treated the structure and logic of the questions on God as well as the initial questions on creation in the *Summa*. The very amiable and far-reaching discussions that resulted during my days at the University of Dallas focused largely on Thomas's Neoplatonism. In consequence, when writing this little book, it seemed that it would be most useful to give a short introduction to his Neoplatonism. This is what is attempted here, where my Aquinas Lecture is supplemented by indications of how Aquinas acquired and used what came to him from the

Neoplatonists: pagan, Jewish, Islamic, and Christian.

The subject of my Aquinas Lecture came out of my seminar for 2012–13 in the Dalhousie University Classics Department. It treated the first forty-five questions of the *Summa theologiae* and my monograph on them, *God in Himself. Aquinas's Doctrine of God as Expounded in the "Summa Theologiae,"* for which my research had been finished thirty years earlier. We looked together at it and at the intervening scholarship, a good deal of it published by me. Public lectures, seminars, and discussions in the fall of 2013 and the winter of 2014 at the Philosophy Department of St. Thomas University, Fredericton, the Classics Department of Princeton University, and the Faculty of Theology and Religious Studies at McGill University, all helped me to come to a clearer understanding of a text I first spoke about in terms of Neoplatonism in Cologne in 1977. It took that long for me to get through the trees to see the shape of the forest—the consolation for my slowness is to have spent so much time in theological contemplation through Thomas's

inexhaustible text. Because mostly I am re-
flecting here on the overall result of Thomas's
arguments and of my previously published
scholarship, I shall generally give bibliograph-
ical indications instead of exhaustive citations.
This will be an introduction.

In the course of my studies, travels, teaching, discussions, lectures, and publications
over more than forty years of work on
Aquinas, I have acquired unpayable debts. In
partial recompense I dedicate this little book
to my students past and present, many of
whom have become my hosts at the universi-
ties where they now teach, and to the Philosophy Department of the University of Dallas,
and especially to its open-minded faculty and
graduate students in that center of independent thought where the dangerously radical
Angelic Doctor would feel at home. There,
admirably, and against the current, the Lib-
eral Arts thrive by way of a carefully constructed and well tested core curriculum of
which the Neoplatonists would have ap-
proved. Within the framework of a religious
collegium, theoria is ethical anagogy oriented
to Wisdom.

I am deeply grateful to Evan King for reading and correcting this text and its parts several times and for the excellent suggestions he has made both out of his extensive scholarship and his literary sense. The lavish hospitality and gracious welcome of the Philosophy Department at the University of Dallas, especially of Professor Philipp Rosemann, the exciting and frank discussions I had with students during my visit, and the courageous efforts of Professor Walz to make my lecture intelligible are all remembered with thanks.

CHAPTER ONE
What Is Neoplatonism? And What Does Aquinas Take from Neoplatonism?

Neoplatonism

"Everyone today is a Neoplatonist," remarked Jean-Marc Narbonne with self-conscious but defensible hyperbole. The longest- lived, most synthetic, and inclusively diverse movement unifying philosophy, religion, the spiritual and moral disciplines, and culture continues to assume ever new forms. By Aquinas's time it looked back from its defining hermeneutic in Plotinus to Pythagoras, Parmenides, Heraclitus, Socrates, Plato, Aristotle, the Stoics and Cynics, Cicero, Philo, Clement, Origen, and

Porphyry, and looked forward to Ambrose, Iamblichus, Augustine, Gregory of Nyssa, Nemesius, Syrianus, Proclus, Ammonius, Simplicius, Macrobius, Boethius, Dionysius, Eriugena, Honorius, Anselm, and the Victorines. By combining the Peripatetics and later Neoplatonists, it would pass on to Ibn Sīnā (Avicenna) writing in Persian and Arabic, to Jews and other Muslims working in Arabic, and to Byzantine Christians writing in Greek, most notably, Philoponus, John of Damascus, al-Fārābī, and the authors of the *Liber de causis*, al-Ghazālī, Moses Maimonides, and even, for some doctrines, Ibn Rushd (Averroës). Directly, by way of translations, and in dialogue with Albert, Bonaventure, and the "Latin Averroists" of the faculty of arts, Neoplatonic treatises, commentaries, fragments and notions were passed on influentially, and sometimes with the highest philosophical and theological authority, to Aquinas. This is a very incomplete list, featuring those in one way or another known to him.

In antiquity, especially with and after Iamblichus and Proclus, Neoplatonists attempted to bring Hellenic philosophies,

especially those of Plato and Aristotle, as well
as Hellenic and the venerable "barbarian" re-
ligions into concord and to reconcile philosophy, religion, and mysticism. Inclusive and
diverse systems resulted. In fact, Neoplatonism must be named in the plural. Two directions emerged from Plotinus, both have
Christian forms, and Aquinas is among their
heirs. Both the direction taken by Augustine
in the wake of Porphyry, and that taken by
Dionysius the Areopagite in the wake of
Iamblichus and Proclus come down to
Aquinas; indeed, they constitute primary
poles of his thinking.

From Simplicius, the sixth-century Neoplatonic historian of philosophy and commentator on Aristotle, Aquinas received a pair of
differing philosophical directions which ex-
haust the possibilities. Aquinas, following
Simplicius, associated them with Plato and
Aristotle, but they also serve to characterize
the two Neoplatonisms. The one, coming
from Plotinus to Augustine and his followers,
the inner journey by way of intellectual intuition, belongs to Platonism for him. The other,
coming from Iamblichus and Proclus via

Dionysius and the *Liber de causis*, passing through the sensible to the invisible, is Aristotle's way. Aquinas writes in his late *Disputed Questions on Spiritual Creatures* (1267–68):

> The diversity of these two positions stems from this, that some, in order to seek the truth about the nature of things, have proceeded from intelligible reasons, and this was the particular characteristic of the Platonists. Some, however, have proceeded from sensible things, and this was the particular characteristic of the philosophy of Aristotle, as Simplicius says in his commentary upon the *Categories*.[1]

To understand the influence of Proclean Neoplatonism on Aquinas, it must be remembered that Proclus comes to him through the

---

1   Aquinas, *Quaestio disputata de spiritualibus creaturis*, art. 3, resp. Aquinas appears to be referring to the prologue of Simplicius's commentary.

Liber de causis (masked as the cap of Aristotle's system, until Aquinas reads the *Elements of Theology* sometime after 1268), and through what is for Aquinas the quasi-apostolic writings of Dionysius the Areopagite. Aquinas supposes that the latter contain the wisdom passed on by St. Paul, who had been elevated to a vision of the spiritual mysteries. They are reconciled to one another and Aristotle by his teacher St. Albert, whose commentaries on the Dionysian corpus Aquinas helped prepare by comparing Latin translations (we have interlinear notes in his telltale illegible script). Given the authority of Aristotle and (indirectly) St. Paul, Aquinas generally (though not always) fits Augustine's Platonism within his Proclean Neoplatonism rather than the other way round. In fact, this is the usual relation the two are given in the Middle Ages, when, beginning with Boethius and Eriugena, both are known.

Plotinus himself shows us the inclusivity of the new form he gives Platonism. Consider for a moment his three primary divine subsistences: the One-Good, Mind, Soul. Plotinus's interpretation of Plato so as to unite the Good

beyond thought and being of the *Republic*
with the One–Non-Being of the *Parmenides*,
together with his understanding of other dialogues so as to cohere with this, may be taken
as the defining move that results in his new
Platonism. It includes the first principle, the
One–Good, which he calls the Father. Thomas
will not follow him here; he will reject Proclus
and Eriugena where they go along with Plotinus on this point, and he will misinterpret
Dionysius in order to prevent having to do so.
Nonetheless, as I hope to show later, his doctrine of God as pure *esse* is affected by the Plotinian One.

Plotinus's second divinity, Mind, he takes
from Aristotle, though understanding it
through the second hypothesis of Plato's *Parmenides*, the One–Being or "One–Many."
This is closer to Aquinas's (and Augustine's)
first principle. If Aristotle permanently gains
a place within this new Platonism through this
move (and by many other essentials like the
notions of actuality and potentiality), Stoicism, deprived of its corporeal monism,
shows itself most clearly with the third divinity, Soul, the "One and Many." Beautiful

Plotinian pictures of the life of nature derive from the Stoics, just as do accounts of the virtues. Augustine owes much to these, perhaps most notably his *rationes seminales*, the "rational seeds" planted by God in the act of creation out of which all emerges over time.

If Augustine helps to show us what of Stoicism belongs in Neoplatonism (and what is excluded), he also makes clearer than anyone how much it and Plotinus depend on skepticism. Engagement with the "Academics" is a constant for Augustine; it begins from the first dialogues, is found at the height of the *De Trinitate*, and is the way into Neoplatonism and the Christian God in the *Confessions*. Skepticism brings him to the self as the fulcrum of knowing because of its balanced equipoise without a reason to move. (The best description of this skeptical situation is found in Augustine's *Confessions* V.) Augustine's move inward, explicitly following the Platonists, is a requirement of this beginning and was the norm for the Augustinian Latin world where Aquinas worked and which he confronted. Thomas did not judge that our knowing had the immediate access to the noetic which Augustine's solution required and his critique required reason to take the opposite way to truth. In this way he is an heir of a different Neoplatonic response to the skeptical turn; his way was Proclean and Dionysian rather than Plotinian and Augustinian. Nonetheless, both ways beyond skepticism share common ground. No one understood better than Aquinas that how a philosophy proceeds depends on the account of the self from which it begins. He unfailingly reminds us of the limitations of our form of knowing while drawing out completely the consequences of his understanding of the human self.

Thus, we might describe Neoplatonism as a return to the content of the philosophies of Plato and Aristotle by way of the skeptical criticism of dogmatic assertions of the power of human knowing, especially, but not exclusively, Stoic and earlier Platonic ones. In sum, if we were to call Aquinas a Neoplatonist—which is not exactly correct in my view—we would expect to find him to be also partly an Aristotelian, partly a Stoic, and partly a skeptic—as indeed we do.

Aquinas's Neoplatonic Doctrines

We can list some of Thomas's borrowings from Middle and Neo-Platonism, starting with those he acquired from the *Liber de causis*. Many of its doctrines he also found in the writings of Dionysius the Areopagite. Together with his colleagues at Paris, where the *Liber* was on the university list of the books of Aristotle for lecture, he had supposed for most of his working life that the *Liber* was the cap of Aristotle's system; the propositions, if not perhaps the commentary on them, were by the authority he called *Philosophus*, "the Philosopher." From the beginning of his writing, the following four Neoplatonic philosophical principles were derived from the *Liber* and credited to the Philosopher:

1) Every secondary cause is only a cause through the primary cause.
2) A thing is known according to the mode of the knower.
3) What knows its essence has complete return upon itself.

4) The first of created things is *esse*, which is the most proper effect of God.

It is crucial to note that after Aquinas came to think that the *Liber* was not by Aristotle but consisted of propositions and ideas taken from Proclus's *Elements of Theology* by Arabic philosophers, there was no change in his use of what he had learned from it—although of course he ceased crediting them to the Philosopher.

Vincent Guagliardo has compiled a list of what Aquinas took over from the *Liber de Causis* and its monotheistic Neoplatonism.[2] I have modified his list, left out items covered above, and continued my numbering:

5) The first being is the "cause of causes."
6) God as the first cause is most intimately present in all things.
7) The higher a cause is, the more extensive and intensive are its effects.
8) The simpler a cause is, the greater and more unlimited is its power.

2   See Aquinas, *Commentary on the Book of Causes*, xxx–xxxi.

9) God alone, as pure *esse*, is infinite and is individuated by his own being as "pure goodness."
10) God is above every name and description.
11) God rules all things without being mixed with them.
12) Separated substances (angels), though simple, have essence and existence (which distinguishes them from the First).
13) Separate substances are full of forms.
14) The individual human soul is free from the conditions of matter both in its capacity to subsist and in its material activity of knowing.
15) The human soul is on the "horizon" of the eternal and above the temporal, sharing both worlds.
16) "All is in all." One thing can be in another as a cause and an effect are in each other.

Still, the list of Aquinas's Neoplatonic principles, doctrines, orderings, and hermeneutical determinations goes on. Most of the following (as well as of the foregoing) he found in writings he attributed to

Dionysius the Areopagite. I continue the numbering from above. 17) One has the nature of the principle. All comes out from unity and returns to it. 18) Nothing exists which does not participate in unity. 19) Indeed, every effect is turned around towards its cause. The structure of reality is remaining, *exitus* and *reditus*; thus, this is the structure of a properly ordered *Summa theologiae.* 20) The *lex divinitatis*—"the highest part of the lower reaches to the lowest part of the higher" derived from Iamblichus—Aquinas attributes to Dionysius and uses it to govern spiritual mediation: the highest only draws the lowest back to itself through a middle. This idea is central to Aquinas's understanding of hierarchy and of the relations of the secular and sacred. 21) The language of emanation—*emanatio*, *diffusio*, *effusio*, *processio*—describes how the Persons come forth within God and how creation comes from them as their common act. 22) Creation is a real relation only in the creature and is its total dependence on God.

23) God cannot be comprehended by anything. 24) God is named from creatures as

from his effects, but in himself he is unknowable. 25) Negative predications of God are truer than affirmative ones. 26) God knows the negative through the positive, evil through the good. 27) God as creator and illuminator is likened Platonically to the radiating sun and is above being and thought. Aquinas himself will prefer, following Aristotle, to liken God's knowing activity in us to light in a medium, but he employs both images. 28) God is above being, in the sense that he is not a being. 29) In this life the soul is joined to God as to the unknown. 30) Humans properly know by ratiocination, moving from one thing to another, and by gathering knowledge from the sensible. 31) Divine things cannot be manifested to humans except under sensible likenesses.

32) The good is diffusive and communicative of itself. 33) All things seek the good. Good extends to being and non-being, but being extends only to existences. 34) Aquinas adopts against the Peripatetics the Platonic and Neoplatonic doctrine of providence, that it extends to the least of things. In the wake of Plotinus, Iamblichus, Proclus, and Ammonius,

and under the direct influence of Boethius, Aquinas distinguishes between providence as God's simple plan (either in God or God Himself) and governance (the same plan multiplied and divided in secondary causes and things). 35) Aquinas takes from Dionysius the Proclean teaching that evil is parasitical on the good and thus has no substantial existence; matter is neither evil nor the cause of evil. 36) Love is an ecstatic and unitive force. Here Aquinas unites Dionysius and Augustine.

37) For Aquinas, it is necessary to side with the Platonists against the Peripatetics on the kinds of spiritual substances and on the determination of their numbers. The multitude of the angels transcends the needs of the material world, so that it cannot be determined by it in the manner of Aristotle. 38) Separate substances are ordered hierarchically. 39) The higher separated substances participate in more universal knowledge than the lower do; they know more than the lower do and direct the lower members of the hierarchy. 40) Spiritual substances have essence, power, and activity as their fundamental structure. 41) Spiritual life moves from

purgation to illumination and from illumination to perfection or union.

We must also include the following points among Thomas's *Neoplatonica*: 42) Platonic language and ideas are appropriate to the spiritual realm, if not to the natural world, where Aristotelian science reigns. 43) In line with Simplicius, Aquinas criticizes Aristotle and the Peripatetics on how to interpret Plato, who, as a theologian using poetic forms of language, is not to be understood literally. 44) Aquinas works within a relation between the natural—philosophy's realm— and the supernatural realm of graciously revealed religion first sketched by Iamblichus. In Aquinas this becomes a mutual relation of philosophical and revealed theology probably developed in reaction against Averroës, and in accord with how Moses Maimonides stood vis-à-vis al-Fārābī, Avicenna, and al-Ghazālī. 45) Intimately connected to this, Thomas uses a Plotinian-Porphyrian-Iamblichan understanding of the hierarchy of the virtues and of their existence in the supra-human spiritual realms. 46) He reconciles Platonic reminiscence and Aristotelian abstraction in the wake of Syrianus. This is fundamental to his doctrine of abstraction and the character and role of the agent intellect. 47) Aquinas uses the reconciliation of Aristotle and Plato wrought by the Neoplatonists to attribute life to God by way of the notion of "motionless motion." For him Plato teaches that God moves himself as "the act of the perfect." 49) Aquinas uses the same reconciliation wrought by the Neoplatonists to attribute both creation from nothing to Plato and Aristotle, and the notion that they both teach the emanation of universal being by way of participation in simple *esse*. 50) By way of Avicenna, and in accord with Augustine, Aquinas explicates the *exitus* of the persons of the Trinity using the law that "from a simple one only a one can come."

By turning more completely to what Thomas took from Porphyry, Augustine, Boethius, Eriugena, the Arabic Peripatetics (who had thoroughly absorbed Neoplatonism), and the late ancient Greek commentators, we could expand this list. However, it now contains enough to explicate the treatise on God of the *Summa theologiae*. In consequence, we shall leave it incomplete and turn to three other questions: How does Aquinas do the history of philosophy? How does he understand it? Is Aquinas a Neoplatonist?

CHAPTER TWO

Aquinas's History of Philosophy; And Is Aquinas a Neoplatonist?

Aquinas as Student of the History of Philosophy

Aquinas is genuinely interested in the history of philosophy: he writes histories and uses them both substantially and polemically, he works hard at it, he has an astonishing ability to root out the meaning of almost unintelligible translations of extremely difficult texts, and he possesses the necessary sympathetic understanding for positions. He has a real critical sense, sometimes approaching philological discipline, thus showing that a theologian can come up to the standards and methods of the faculty of arts. As a result of his changing understanding, his views on very important matters also change. In no area, except for Aristotle and the Peripatetic tradition, does he labor harder or with greater consequence than in his understanding of Platonism. His interpretations of the two traditions develop together, as the traditions themselves did; ultimately his thought becomes more and more Neoplatonic.

We can see the very learned historian doing his philological best in his late *Exposition of the "Liber de causis"* (1272–73). Thomas's insights depend on his use of William of Moerbeke's 1268 translation of Proclus's *Elements of Theology*. After pointing to the fact that the *Liber* was a translation from the Arabic and did not exist in Greek, he painstakingly located its sources in Proclus's *Elements*, which he notes was translated from the Greek, and he works out how Proclus had been both adopted and modified. He compares Proclus, as the acme of Platonism, to the Dionysian *corpus*, the *Liber*, Aristotle, and the Christian faith. With this addition to his knowledge of the Greek fount of philosophy, he continued more sure-footedly and determinedly with the conciliation of Platonism and Aristotle for the sake of truth, both philosophical and religious. This was the project, conscious or unconscious, explicit or implicit, of most of the commentators he knew, including Averroës.

From Averroës, Thomas derived one of the results of this conciliation, which he used early and often, namely, the "motionless motion" by which God can appropriately be called "living." This notion originates from interpreting a passage of the *De anima* probably intended to oppose Plato's notion of the soul as self-moving. In the *Sentences Commentary* (1252–54) and other early works, Aquinas takes up Augustine's use of the *large* sense of motion when it refers to intellectual life, and he explains what Augustine means through Plato, as represented by Averroës.[1]

1   See Aquinas, *In quatuor libros Sententiarum*, lib.

In his evolving descriptions of Dionysius's philosophical affiliation, we have a clear example of how Aquinas sees the relation of philosophy and Christian doctrine, how he advances in understanding the history of philosophy, and how he changes his mind as a result. In his *Sentences Commentary*, when determining whether the heavens are of the same elemental nature as the inferior creation, Thomas observes that, before Aristotle, all thought they were identical. After him, "because of the efficacy of his reasons," philosophers agreed and everyone followed Aristotle's opinion. "Similarly, the expositors of Sacred Scripture differed on this matter, according as they were followers of the different philosophers by whom they were educated in philosophical matters." Thus Basil and Augustine and many of the saints followed the opinion of Plato "in philosophical matters which do not regard the faith. Dionysius, however, almost everywhere follows Aristotle,

1, dist. 8, qu. 3, art. 1, ad 2; Aquinas, *Super De Trinitate*, qu. 5, art. 4, obj. 2; Aquinas, *Quaestiones disputatae de veritate*, qu. 23, art. 1, ad 7.

as is clear to those who diligently look into his books."[2]

More than a decade later, in his *Exposition of the "De divinis nominibus"* (1266 and 1268), Aquinas exhibits an altered view and an important advance in his knowledge of Platonism. He discerns how "one" functions as principle of everything. He lists "five modes in which one has the nature (*ratio*) of a principle," identifying two of them as coming from Plato.[3] His understanding of the subordination of all to the One-Good as First Principle in Platonism will keep growing and, among other important consequences, will change his view of Plato. At the end of his writing, Aquinas will bring Plato and Aristotle into complementary concord, correct Aristotle by Plato and Plato by Aristotle, and even restate Aristotle's teaching in Platonic form. Now, earlier, in the *Proemium* to his *Exposition*, Aquinas discerns something else about

2 Aquinas, *In quatuor libros Sententiarum*, lib. 2, dist. 14, qu. 1, art. 2.
3 Aquinas, *In librum beati Dionysii de divinis nominibus*, XIII, ii, §981.

Platonism which will endure, increase in importance, and be crucial to the conciliation of Plato and Aristotle. He sees that the Dionysian "way of speaking" and style, which he characterizes as "obscure," were those used by the Platonists. This is far from being a condemnation and points to another possible concordance.

Platonic reasoning by way of separated abstractions is "neither consonant with the faith nor the truth" when used in respect to natural things; on these, for Aquinas, Aristotle is always right. By contrast, when Platonists speak in this way of "the First Principle of things, they are most true and consonant with Christian faith." Thus, Dionysius is right to speak about God in terms of "goodness, or super-goodness or the principally good, or the goodness of all good."[4] In later works, following Simplicius, Aquinas will tell us that obscure and poetic speech is both Platonic and suitable to theology, but that Aristotle and his followers interpret and refute Plato as though

4   Aquinas, *In De divinis nominibus*, proemium, §2.

he were speaking literally. While Thomas will normally side with Aristotle in the literal dispute, nonetheless room is left for a concord should letter be replaced by intention.

In the *Disputed Question on Spiritual Creatures*, which shows Aquinas's reading of two late ancient Greek commentators, one Peripatetic, the other Neoplatonic—namely, Themistius and Simplicius—he reaffirms his earlier placing of Augustine within the Platonic tradition. Thomas judges: "Augustine followed Plato as much as the Catholic faith would allow."[5] When asking whether the human soul, as spiritual substance, is united to the body through a medium, Thomas's Aristotelian hylomorphism, for which he warred against his contemporary "Augustinians" at great risk, is at stake. Hylomorphism is Aristotle's fundamental idea that all natural sensible substances, including the human, are composed of form and matter, so that the soul is the form of the body—a doctrine deemed dangerous because it puts the immortality of

5   Aquinas, *Quaestio disputata de spiritualibus creaturis*, art. 10, ad 8.

the soul into question. Before he determines the matter "according to the true principles of philosophy which Aristotle considered,"[6] Thomas places the opinions within the schema taken from Simplicius quoted earlier: "Some, in order to seek the truth about the nature of things, have proceeded from intelligible reasons, and this was the particular characteristic of the Platonists. Some, however, have proceeded from sensible things, and this was the particular characteristic of the philosophy of Aristotle."[7] All depends upon whether abstractions exist separately from minds and whether humans have intellectual intuition which can reason down from them. Aquinas accepts neither.

After undertaking his expositions of philosophical works and reconsideration of philosophical questions which he continued to the end of his life, when he was writing the concluding part of his *Disputed Questions on Evil* (1270–71), Aquinas put Augustine and Dionysius together. In a series of replies to

6   Ibid., art. 3, resp.
7   See note 1 above.

objections, he first judges that Augustine spoke about the bodies of demons "as they seemed to some learned persons, that is, the Platonists." According to the logic he took from Simplicius, Thomas then goes on both to affirm and to correct the Platonists on how we know and, finally, declares the philosophical allegiance of the Areopagite: "Dionysius was a follower of the judgments of the Platonists for the most part."[8]

Two or three years later, in his *Exposition of the Book of Causes*, Thomas decides both that its author "seems to follow the judgment of Dionysius" and that Aristotle, the Catholic faith, Dionysius, and this Proclean and Plotinian Arabic author are frequently in accord.[9] The *Treatise on Separate Substances*, written at the same time (1272–73), combines a progressive history of philosophy with a complementary concordance of Aristotle and Platonism in order to establish the truth about

8   Aquinas, *Quaestiones disputatae de malo*, qu. 16, art. 1, ad 1, ad 2, and ad 3.
9   Aquinas, *Super librum De causis expositio*, prop. 4.

the immaterial substances, who are the instruments of revelation and providence.

The movements I have traced exhibit that, for Aquinas, there is from the beginning an intimate relation between philosophy and Christian theology. Philosophical positions and ways of reasoning can be both false and contrary to the faith, and some of the saints follow dangerous philosophical roads. However, philosophy with true principles and convincing reasoning remains and is necessary for the understanding of revelation. After the Greek commentators help him to understand better its dynamic, he will become able to show how philosophy has a shape in which thought is compelled towards truth. He will do this after the manner of Aristotle, but the Stagirite will be read within a much more extensive and generous Neoplatonic vision of the history of philosophy than was Aristotle's own. Because most of Thomas's guides either will be Neoplatonic commentators on Aristotle or, if Arabic Peripatetics, will have reconciled Proclus and Aristotle, philosophical truth for Aquinas will involve an embrace by Aristotle of his teacher, which was beyond the Philosopher's own grasp. What impels the philosophical commentaries devoted to understanding, clarifying, expositing, and testing this true path has appeared. The examples I have given show how philosophical positions transmute, interchange, and complement one another in Thomas's thinking.

From Doxography to History

Et scias, quod non perficitur homo in philosophia nisi ex scientia duarum philosophiarum Aristotelis et Platonis (Albertus Magnus, *Metaphysica*).[10]

The work of a theologian, Thomas's work, is the explication of Sacred Scripture, either in commentary, in disputation, or in writings like his *Summa theologiae*. In consequence,

10 Albertus Magnus, *Metaphysica*, lib. I, tr. 5, cap. 15 (ed. Geyer, Cologne ed. 16/1, p. 89, ll. 85–7): "Man is brought to perfection in philosophy only by knowing the two philosophies of Aristotle and Plato." My thanks to Evan King for this quotation.

one of the greatest, and continuing, puzzles about Aquinas is why he engaged in the study of philosophy I just partly described. Why, from 1267 until 1273, the year before his death, did he take up expositions of the works of Aristotle, including what he had thought was one of them, the *Liber de causis*, as well as polemical writings against Averroistic philosophers in the faculty of arts, leaving unfinished theological works like the *Summa theologiae*?

Part of the answer must come from new means for understanding philosophy that were at Thomas's disposal. From 1260, Thomas's Dominican brother William of Moerbeke undertook a series of translations of Aristotle and of late ancient Greek commentators and philosophers; beginning with Alexander of Aphrodisias's commentaries on the treatises *On Meteors* and *On Sense* by Aristotle, and with Aristotle's own *On the Parts of Animals*, moving on in 1266 to the *Commentary on the Categories* by Simplicius and, in 1267, to the paraphrase of Aristotle's *De anima* by Themistius, in 1268 William of Moerbeke tackled Proclus's *Elements of*

Theology. His translating work would continue after Aquinas's death. These translations enabled Aquinas to get back beyond the Latin and Arabic heirs of Greek philosophy to what were for him the pure sources—something that Averroës, his first guide to Aristotle, also had sought. But opportunity is not reason enough. Why did Aquinas want to know and understand philosophy's beginning?

Moerbeke's translations of Alexander, Themistius, and Simplicius did more than expand Thomas's knowledge of the positions of the philosophers. They enabled him to discern what Jan Aertsen calls "historical progression" in philosophy,[11] compelled, as Aristotle had said, "by the truth itself" to use history as a philosophical argument—something he did very tellingly against Averroistic philosophers in the faculty of arts—and, most importantly in my view, to continue the concordist project of the late ancient schools, especially the Neoplatonic one. Bringing diverse and seemingly opposed positions into an accord that is not merely imposed from outside

11   Aertsen, "Aquinas's Philosophy," 28.

requires discerning the shape of philosophy's internal and, for Aquinas, providential movement. For him, this is the way to find certainty, complementarity, balance, and, as far as it is possible, complete truth. On the basis of Romans 1:20 (the invisible things of God are known from the things he has made), Aquinas believes that this truth is promised by God and that its finding is demanded of us because it is a requirement of sacred doctrine.

For Aquinas's discerning of an "historical progression," Aertsen points us to the question in the *Summa theologiae* on whether prime matter is caused by God. It seems, contrary to the Christian faith—here articulated by Augustine in the *sed contra*—that, as the Aristotelian supposition of all change, prime matter cannot be made (*facta*). However, in fact, "the ancient philosophers advanced in the knowledge of the truth," although "step by step and, as it were, haltingly."[12] Ultimately, by advancing to more and more universal causes, "some" (who certainly

12 Aquinas, *Summa theologiae* I, qu. 44, art. 2, resp.

included for him Aristotle) "climbed to the consideration of being as being (*ens inquantum est ens*)." "So we must posit that even prime matter is caused by the universal cause of beings." Thus, for Thomas, Aristotle has arrived at a condition of creation from nothing and, as Aertsen observes, it "appears as the result of the *internal* development of thought independent of the external aid of revelation."[13]

Another progressive history in the *Summa* brings us to the role of Themistius in constructions of this kind. This one appears when Thomas asks "whether the soul knows bodily things through its own essence." There, when starting with the *antiqui philosophi*, he gives as their principle "like is known by like (*simile simili*)," with the consequence that the object known is in the knower corporeally as it is also in the known. Aquinas follows this with a representation of Plato as moving truth forward by use of the same principle in order to teach, on the contrary, an immaterial knowing with an immaterial separate form as its

13 Aertsen, "Aquinas's Philosophy," 30.

object.[14] That "like is known by like" was a principle of the physicists as Aristotle treats them in his *De anima*.[15] Its new frequent use by Aquinas in his progressive histories constructed in the *Summa* and the *De anima* commentary seems to be explained by its appearance in Themistius.[16]

At the place where the formula occurs in Aristotle and Themistius, Thomas begins his comment by observing that the *antiqui philosophi*, in assuming that the principles of things were in the soul, were "compelled by the truth itself." This notion is found in Aristotle, who in the *Metaphysics* speaks of "the things themselves opening the way and compelling the first philosophers to seek" and of the ancients as "compelled by the truth itself."[17] Similarly, in the *Physics*, he finds the same philosophers "compelled as it were by the truth itself."[18]

14 Aquinas, *Summa theologiae* I, qu. 84, art. 2, resp.
15 See Aristotle, *De anima* I.2, 404b17.
16 Themistius, *Commentaire sur le Traité de l'âme d'Aristote*, Book I, p. 26, l. 10.
17 Aristotle, *Metaphysics* I.3, 984a18 and 984b10.
18 Aristotle, *Physics* I.10, 188b29–30.

Thomas does not fail to notice these compulsions, commenting on them in his expositions of the works. However, in his commentary on the *De anima*, he adds that the physicists "dreamed, as it were, of the truth."[19] Aquinas seems to have intended this "dreaming" to explain why these ancients could not give reasons for what they said and yet were moved upward towards incorporeal causes. Themistius had the same explanation; he wrote that "they seem to dream up this reality—the incorporeal nature, I mean."[20] Thomas may be following Themistius.

Thomas's most detailed progressive history is found in his treatise *On Separate Substances* (that is, angels), which, like his *Exposition of the "Liber de causis,"* depended on Moerbeke's translation of Proclus's *Elements*. Proclus added to the information available for writing a progressive and conciliating history of philosophy and theology—pagan, Jewish, Islamic, and Christian. The first

19 Aquinas, *Sententia libri De anima*, I, iv.
20 Themistius, *Commentaire sur le Traité de l'âme d'Aristote*, Book I, p. 36, ll. 65–6.

chapter of the history concerns "the opinions of the ancients and of Plato." There is a movement forward among the ancients towards the knowledge of separate substance; they get beyond the corporeal gods of the atomists and the Epicurean search for ceaseless pleasures that such deities inspire. Plato does better than his predecessors in dealing with the two errors philosophy must overcome. One is the denial that humans can know with certainty. The second is that nothing exists separate from bodies. Plato solves both errors, solves them together, and his solution is correct insofar as they can be solved only together. However, the connection between knowledge of the truth and the existence of separate substances is not what Plato takes it to be. In order to save knowledge, Plato simply reversed the Physicists, solving the problem too immediately. Plato projected what belongs to our thinking onto an external reality:

> Thus, according to this reasoning, because the intellect when knowing the truth apprehends something beyond the matter of sensible

> things, Plato thought some things
> existed separated from sensible
> things.[21]

For Aquinas, Plato's work is an essential part of the philosophical progress. However, history quickly becomes more complicated. Thomas notes that the *Platonici* posited orders of separate forms upon which intellects depended. Plato is represented as establishing a hierarchy in which mathematicals were intermediate between the forms and sensibles.[22] At the highest level were entities like the good itself, intellect itself, and life itself. Aquinas judges that, in this case, the Platonic error in solving the epistemological dilemma involved a false separation of the object from the subject of intellection. The intellectual realities (*intelligibilia*) were separated from intellects when the "gods, which is what Plato called the separate intelligible forms," were separated from knowing.[23] The philosophical

---

21 Aquinas, *De substantiis separatis*, cap. 1.
22 See ibid.
23 Ibid., cap. 4.

error involved in this separation of subject
and object evidently has religious consequences. Happily, Aristotle did not need separate forms to explain how we know.[24] Thus,
as Thomas judges in his *Exposition* of the
Liber, in this aspect of his teaching on the
kinds of separate substances, Aristotle's par-
simony is "more consonant with the Christian
faith" than is the position of the Platonists.[25]
However, the Platonic tendency to multiply
entities also benefits the truth.

The second chapter of the *De substantiis
separatis* is devoted to the opinion of Aristotle. There Aquinas judges that Aristotle's way
of reasoning, by way of motion, to the existence of separate substances is "more manifest
and more certain."[26] In his commentary on
the *Categories*, Simplicius had also judged the
Aristotelian way to have a more persuasive
necessity for those living at the level of

24 See ibid., cap. 2.
25 Aquinas, *Super De causis*, prop. 10. He makes
    much the same point when commenting on prop.
    13.
26 Aquinas, *De substantiis separatis*, cap. 2. Com-
    pare *ST* I, qu. 2, art. 3, resp.

sensation.[27] There is, however, a deficiency in Aristotle's alternative way. What is defective matches its virtue. His staying "with what does not depart much from what is evident to sense" gives a greater certainty to our rational knowledge of the existence of separate substances. It shows its limits, however, when determining their kinds and numbers. On this, Aristotle's position seems "less sufficient than the position of Plato."[28] By limiting separate substances to the two kinds needed to move the heavens, and with their numbers tied to the same necessity, he fails to account for the spirits who possess us and of whom sorcerers dispose; in addition, by tying the number of the angels to the necessities of what is beneath them, he has reversed the proper order of reasoning.

In Simplicius's commentary on the *Categories*, another formula for relating Plato and Aristotle can be found. It comes to mind at this point because Simplicius's implied

27 See Simplicius, *Commentaire sur les Catégories*, i, prologus, p. 8, l. 74–p. 9, l. 79.
28 Aquinas, *De substantiis separatis*, cap. 2.

criticism of Aristotle here is Aquinas's own in respect to the number and kinds of spiritual creatures:

> [Aristotle] always refuses to deviate from nature; on the contrary, he considers even things that are above nature, according to their relation to nature, just as, by contrast, the divine Plato, according to Pythagorean usage, examines even natural things insofar as they participate in the things above nature.[29]

As the treatise advances, the agreements of Plato and Aristotle are considered in the same way as their complementary differences had been. We cannot dilate on these but we must not fail to consider an accord between Plato and Aristotle, one that we have noted before, which involves both the ongoing change in Aquinas's view of Plato and a clearly Platonic

29 Simplicius, *On Aristotle Categories 1–4*, 6.1.27–30. Cf. M. Chase, "The Medieval Posterity of Simplicius' Commentary on the *Categories*," 16.

representation of what both Aristotle and Plato think. This is their agreement on the creation of all things by a single First Principle.

In *On Separate Substances*, Thomas reports:

> According to the opinion of Plato and Aristotle ... it is necessary beyond the mode of coming to be, by which something becomes by the coming of form to matter, to presuppose another origin of things, according as *esse* is bestowed on the whole universe of things by a first being that is its own being.[30]

This creation *ex nihilo* is not contradicted by the fact that Plato and Aristotle held immaterial substances and the heavenly bodies to have always existed. Aquinas does not judge that the eternal existence of a creature and its being a creature are incompatible. In consequence, he declares Plato and Aristotle did not on this account deny a cause of their eternal being; indeed, they did not "deviate in this from the

---

30   Aquinas, *De substantiis separatis*, cap. 9.

doctrine of Catholic faith" by positing uncreated things.[31] He states the doctrine that God is the sole cause of being for all things in a form which is more Platonic than Aristotelian. The First Principle is called *simplicissimum*, and Thomas argues that "because subsistent being must be one ... it is necessary that all other things which are under it exist in the way they do as participants in *esse*."[32]

His exposition of the *Liber de causis* shows that, having looked at Plato more and more in Neoplatonic terms, Thomas saw that, for Platonists, all is derived from one exalted First Principle from which being comes. Even if the Platonists "posited many gods ordered under one" rather than, as we do, "positing one only having all things in itself," everyone agrees "universality of causality belongs to God."[33] The Platonic language betrays what underlies this concordance here.

The notion that Aristotle taught a doctrine of creation was developed among the late

31 Ibid., cap. 9.
32 Ibid.
33 Aquinas, *Super De causis*, prop. 19.

NEOPLATONISM IN THE *SUMMA THEOLOGIAE* ON GOD

antique conciliators of Plato and Aristotle. The Neoplatonists wanted to draw together the pagan Genesis—the *Timaeus*—and its Demi-urge with Aristotle's *Physics* and his Unmoved Mover. To do this they needed to find some way of reconciling Aristotle's eternal universe with that in the *Timaeus*, which, as Aquinas had discerned in his *Commentary on the "De Caelo"* (composed just before *On Separate Substances*), is generated and corruptible, al-though perpetual because it is held in being by the divine will.[34] The efforts and diverse posi-tions of the ancient commentators gave rise to the pervasive notion in late antiquity and in the Middle Ages that Aristotle and Plato regarded the First Principle as a creator. Aquinas and his Aristotle are the heirs to this notion.

Is Aquinas a Neoplatonist?

So is Aquinas a Neoplatonist? This is not the same as asking whether he would call himself

34 Aquinas, *Sententia De caelo et mundo*, I, xxiii, §
    236; I, xxix, § 283.

one, but I think that in the end his judgment and ours can be the same, or at least close to one another. Let us then ask first how he would categorize his philosophy—or, in his words, which philosopher he follows.

Of course, there is no "Neoplatonism" for Aquinas; it is an invention of the eighteenth century, by those wishing to distinguish the Platonism of the perennial tradition from what they found in the dialogues of Plato. When all is said and done, Aquinas knows almost nothing about the Plato of the dialogues. He learns about Platonism first from Aristotle and Augustine, who selectively report doctrines identified as Platonist, albeit often misrepresented and supplied with their criticisms. He really gets the Platonic arguments near the end of his writing when he reads Proclus's *Elements of Theology*, which was the acme of Platonism for Aquinas. Its doctrines had in fact deeply influenced his thinking right from the beginning. Now he knows their source and their rational basis. So our first question becomes: Does Aquinas believe he is following Plato as he has learned about his teaching and as that teaching finds its most revealing exposition in Proclus? The answer to that question is given in his *Exposition of the "Liber de causis,"* and it is both yes and no. Yes, because he recognizes in the *Elements* the source of what he accepted from the *Liber de causis* and used as philosophical principles and doctrines throughout his life. Yes, because he also recognizes the consonance of the *Elements* with what he took and used under the authority of Dionysius. But the answer is also no, partly because he misunderstands both Proclus and Dionysius on the nature of the First Principle—where he thinks Aristotle is right. No again, because, as his histories show, although he judged that Plato was essential to the progress of truth, he did not get everything right. Happily, where Plato got things wrong, Aristotle usually (but not always) got them right. And still more happily, where Aristotle got them wrong, Platonism was there to provide a better understanding. Does this mean, then, that Aquinas would regard philosophy in general, and his philosophical positions in particular, as an eclectic jumble, something chosen from here, something else from there? To this we can give a definite no. Philosophy has a history that lives under the compulsion of the truth of things—that is to say, under God's guidance. That truth is concordist.

Let us call to mind how truth works for Aquinas, in the *Summa theologiae*, in the Church, and in philosophy: it becomes known through one-sided error and its consequent conflict, through the yes and no, the *sic et non*. The truthful determination is not choosing between the two sides; that is what lawyers and sophists do. Judges and philosophers find the middle that respects the partial truth in both sides; moreover, because the determination is itself partial, it leads to further questions. This Neoplatonists know because the One-Good is not graspable in itself; only its always partial manifestations are known, and nothing else is known or is knowable in this life.

So Aquinas is a Neoplatonist insofar as he holds what he—and usually (but far from always) we—regard as Platonist developments and doctrines. Leaving aside Aristotle's identification of himself as a Platonist, Aquinas is not self-consciously a Platonist when he adopts what he regards as Aristotle's positions

or ways of thinking, although we might identify Aquinas as a Neoplatonist in many of
these as well. Finally, he is a Neoplatonist in
seeking a concord with Aristotle and the real
(a qualification he would require) Peripatetics.
But then, they sought the same. On both sides
the place of concord is the place of truth.

CHAPTER THREE
Sacred Teaching: Preliminary Considerations in the First Question of the *Summa Theologiae*

Whether besides the Philosophical Disciplines Another Teaching is Necessary

Aquinas's *Summa theologiae* opens with a revolutionary question which he was the first to ask. Its supposition and answer determine the mutual relation of philosophy and revealed theology in his thought, have the greatest consequences for the future of philosophy and theology in the West, and set up the first of the circles this book will consider. The question itself concedes what Thomas's conservative adversaries most feared, a reality they refused to admit.

The first article of the first question of the first part of his most influential work, the one where he was able for the first time to give theology what he conceived to be its proper order, is this: "whether besides the philosophical disciplines another teaching is necessary." The question assumes a true knowledge based in the natural powers of reason; it asks whether this is all humans should and can know, and whether there is need and room for any other kind of knowledge than the philosophical "disciplines."

Sacred doctrine sets itself the task of finding a place and a necessity for itself relative to assumed natural human knowledge and powers enabling humans to construct a world aiming for—and, in an important sense, achieving—knowledge even of God. The arguments in the objections used to set up the problem establish a philosophy independent of and sufficient without gracious revelation. The God of the "theology which is part of philosophy" would be the foundation for and, as contemplated, the beatifying conclusion of right reason. Revealed doctrine must justify itself in the face of an assumed philosophically constructed theoretical world. The paradigm Aquinas established, in the face of these assumptions, for the relations between philosophy and what is supernaturally revealed (or "known by the light of divine revelation") is so influential that it has become normal to look at what preceded him through it, an anachronistic distortion.

Because we generally assume a world constructed by what at present corresponds to the theoretical and practical disciplines, and by what Aquinas qualifies as "philosophical," it is almost impossible for us to appreciate the shocking character of Thomas's question to a Western Christian in the thirteenth century. The Latin West was dominated by Augustine and by those self-consciously in his tradition who successfully opposed Aquinas's innovations during his life and immediately afterwards. As a result, positions he maintained were officially condemned by the ecclesiastical authorities during and following the last years of his life. The Augustinians, led by Franciscans, were the normative theologians of the thirteenth century, not Aquinas. For the Augustinians, philosophy and Christian faith were to be identical in content if not in form. Reason had not the independence from revelation which would permit it to say anything other than what faith believed, not even something less. The notion that the teaching based on faith might have to justify itself relative to an autonomously established reason with a complete account of all that is was both unthinkable and frightening.

The first objection, the first argument in the whole system, proposes that whatever is not above reason is sufficiently treated in the philosophical disciplines. "Therefore, besides them, there is no need of any further knowledge." The philosophical sciences providing this complete account are usually attributed to Aristotle and, indeed, "the Philosopher" is spoken of in the second objection when his *Metaphysics* is cited to the effect that there is a philosophical science of God. In fact, however, the philosophical disciplines with a complete account of reality are established over and against what revelation might know, because of the systematization of philosophical sciences in the Peripatetic and Neoplatonic schools of later antiquity, on the one hand, and because of the Islamic Arabic mediation of Aristotle to the Latins, on the other. Arabic philosophy assumed this systematization and added to it an opposition between the whole content of intellect as known conceptually in reason and that same content apprehended by representation, the power which enabled prophecy and imaginative persuasion. As Alain de Libera puts it, the Arabs mediated the texts of Aristotle to the Latins as "a total philosophic corpus, into which the whole of Hellenistic thought, profoundly Neoplatonized, had surreptitiously crept."[1]

Within the Islamic Arabic world the last great defender of the need for and certainty of a complete philosophical knowledge of what

1   Alain de Libera, *Penser au moyen âge* (Paris: Seuil, 1991), 20.

is was Averroës. Aquinas calls him "the Commentator" because of the authority that his commentaries on the works of Aristotle enjoyed in the Latin world. If Averroës comes to mind in the objections of the first article, Moses Maimonides, his Jewish twelfth-century contemporary also from Cordoba in Spain, appears in Thomas's response. His *Guide to the Perplexed*, which, while accepting both orientations, aimed to deal with what was opposing in the demands on a Jew who was simultaneously a conscientious follower of the Law and had been successful at philosophy, was known to Aquinas from the beginning of his systematic writing. The problems of Maimonides's disciple resemble those of the Latin theologian most authoritative for Aquinas, Augustine (he and Dionysius share the prizes for the most numerous citations of Christian theologians by Aquinas). Plotinus supplied Augustine both with a positive conception of immaterial substance and the way to arrive at it, namely, by interior self-knowledge. Aquinas, by contrast, adopts his way for arriving at the same end from Aristotle, from the Arabic philosophical melding of Proclus and Aristotle, and from what is Proclean in Dionysius. For all four—Aristotle, Proclus, Dionysius, and Aquinas—the human soul was turned by nature to the sensible and was not capable of immediate self-knowledge. As I have indicated above, when Plotinian-Augustinian Neoplatonism conflicts with the Proclean-Dionysian sort, Aquinas opts for the second and places the first within it systematically.

A Theologian in the "City of Philosophers"[2]

With Aquinas, following in the footsteps of his great teacher Albert, for the first time in the Latin Middle Ages, a theologian engaged the philosophers on their own terrain as a separate, limited, subordinate sphere, with its own proper methods and autonomy. Thomas, in opposition both to the Aristotle of Averroës and

2   This is what Albert called the faculty of arts; see Aertsen, "Aquinas's Philosophy," 24.

to the Augustinians, makes a humbled but quasi-autonomous philosophy into the servant of revealed theology. Agreeing with Maimonides that what philosophy demonstrated with certainty revelation could not contradict, he agrees equally that, where reason left matters open, Scripture revealed things necessary to reaching the happiness for which God created us.[3] He adopts the approach taken by Maimonides, who faced the same kind of adversaries to his left and his right—namely, Arabic philosophy, on the one hand, and the Islamic and Jewish dialectical theology that Maimonides identified as shared by and originating with the Christians, on the other. Aquinas judges the demand of his Augustinian adversaries that things only faith could know (such as the temporal beginning of the world; a universal, individual, and immediate providence; the Trinity; and the Incarnation—the first two items on this list are also on Maimonides's) be rationally proven only brought destructive disrepute to both theology and philosophy.

3   Aquinas, *In quatuor libros Sententiarum*, lib. 2, dist. 1, qu. 1, art. 5, resp. and ad sed contra.

Thomas's Neoplatonism emerges when he credits Dionysius with the notion that, for humans, revelation is normally given in sensible symbols, images, and signs wherein sacred intelligible and superintelligible realities are adapted to the form of our knowing by being thus veiled.[4] Revelation comes to believers in scriptural images and narratives which, uncorrected, deceive them into believing divinity to be multiple, corporeal, composite, and subject to passions. Maimonides and Aquinas both inherit the tradition of philosophical theology coming from the pre-Socratic and Platonic criticism of mythic accounts of the gods. Plato's standards for purifying poetic theology were radically intensified by his Neoplatonic successors, of whom Aquinas is an heir; the corporeality, division, mutability, potentiality, and causing of evil ascribed to God in Scripture must be understood as signifying their opposites. In consequence, the philosophical climb by which we can see the truth about spiritual substance that Scripture reveals is both necessary and meritorious. The power of

4   See *ST* I, qu.1, art. 9 and qu. 3, art. 1, ad 1.

mind is increased corporately and individually by reaching higher levels of abstraction, by our rising to and becoming one with higher levels of reality. All these points are made in the first question of the *Summa*.

For Aquinas it belongs to our "natural perfection" to know God from creatures and by abstraction from sensible things. The ladder of the philosophical sciences constitutes them as preambles by which the human mind gains the strength for proving the existence of God with irrefutable certainty,[5] for knowing both his negative attributes—simplicity, immutability, eternity, etc.—and (in the very limited measure of which it is capable) the divine mysteries standing both above scientific reason and even beyond the metaphysical wisdom toward which reason ascends. Revealed theology based on God's own self-knowledge needs philosophy, not because of what God's knowledge lacks, but because of our human deficiency.

Like his Neoplatonic predecessors, Thomas is always aware that our theology, though valid because it participates in higher

5   Aquinas, *De veritate*, qu. 10, art. 12.

forms of knowledge, nonetheless belongs to
human reason. By its labor of abstraction,
human science exercises our minds in the
knowledge of intellectual objects separated
from matter that theology needs. Without philosophy—or, in any case, without the rise of
our minds to conceptual thought—we would
not understand divine speech.[6] When arguing
against Anselm and the Augustinians that
God's existence is not self-evident, he reminds
us that humans have even thought that God
was a body.[7]

Given that the rise to conceptual thinking,
which the philosophical disciplines effect, is
necessary for our right understanding of God
and that knowing God is proper to him alone,
it is not surprising that Aquinas supposes philosophy to be a kind of revelation: "the study
of philosophy is in its own right allowable and
praiseworthy, because God revealed to the
philosophers the truth which they perceive, as
Romans 1 says."[8] He understands Aristotle

6   See *ST* I, qu. 1, art. 5, ad 2.
7   See *ST* I, qu. 2, art. 1, ad 2.
8   *ST* II-II, qu. 167, art. 1, ad 3.

and Plato to teach this so far as they maintain that our knowledge of God is a participation in the divine self-knowing. This doctrine, which Aquinas finds in the *Metaphysics* as well in as the *Nicomachean Ethics*, he takes to be the condition of metaphysics as knowledge of divinity.[9] Grace does not destroy nature; it brings it to completion.[10]

In *ST* 1.1.1, Aquinas is concerned with the reasons we need instruction by divine revelation "even in respect to those things about God which human reason is able to investigate." In the *Disputed Questions on Truth*, when he is considering whether it is necessary to have faith, he acknowledges his debt to "the five reasons which Rabbi Moses [Maimonides] gives."[11] In their common

---

9   See Aquinas, *Sententia libri Metaphysicorum* 1.3, 18–20; Aquinas, *Sententia libri Ethicorum* 10.11.

10 See *ST* I, qu. 1, art. 8, ad 2: "... gratia non tollat naturam, sed perficiat."

11 Aquinas, *De veritate* 14.10; also see Aquinas, *Summa contra gentiles* 1.4. The "five reasons" occur in Maimonides, *Guide of the Perplexed* 1.34.

judgments about the difficulty of theology and about the necessity of keeping it from all except mature students with long preparation both moral and intellectual, Aquinas and Maimonides were following Plato, Aristotle, the curricula of the Neoplatonic schools, and their predecessors in the Arabic philosophical tradition. The abstractness of philosophy generally, and of metaphysics particularly, the weakness of our minds which must be strengthened by mathematical and other studies, the extent of the ground which must be covered to reach it, the length of time it takes to traverse this, the need for developed moral virtues and the proper temperament: these are all reasons we require the gift of supernatural revelation.

Nonetheless, in the course of showing the inadequacies of natural reason for attaining the ultimate human happiness, Aquinas actually strengthens it. As against Augustinians, for him sacred doctrine is not fundamentally practical or affective but theoretical, and we are saved by knowing truths which philosophical reason unaided by grace cannot know: "We must know an end before we direct our intentions and actions towards that end. Therefore, it is necessary for human salvation that some truths which exceed human reason be known through divine revelation."[12] We are related to an end beyond reason in such a way that revelation strengthens our reason and will by giving them truths to know and goods to love higher than their natural capacities reach. The infusion of grace perfects the rational power: "Grace does not destroy nature; it brings it to completion."[13] The natural light by which we know, the agent intellect, is a participation by us in God's own knowing, his uncreated light.[14]

Aquinas places moral virtue and philosophical reason within systematic structures derived by way of lengthy mediation from Porphyry and Iamblichus. In consequence, although the overarching theological and religious framework is for the sake of what philosophy cannot attain, for Thomas as well as for pagan Neoplatonists, philosophy is a

12   *ST* I, qu. 1, art. 1.
13   *ST* I, qu. 1, art. 8, ad 2.
14   See my essay "*Participatio divini luminis*."

way of life which transforms us towards de-iformity. Iamblichus introduces the notion of the supernatural into theology; supernature presupposes nature.[15] Like Aquinas, the "divine" Iamblichus is all at once a ritualistic priest, a theologian, and a philosopher. Working within the tradition of Neoplatonic systematic theology, Aquinas shares the aim of maintaining the difference, the integrity, and the connection of (1) sacramental practices in which the divine and humans cooperate; (2) human moral discipline; (3) the rational and human work of philosophy culminating in contemplation of God; and (4) our passive yielding to the gracious activity of the divine toward us. Our knowing and loving ascent to God is by the meeting of two movements; two circles, one rising from creation toward God, the other descending from the divine, become one.

The final word in *ST* 1.1.1 continues to provide a place for revealed knowledge without negating the truth and completeness of the human sciences as human, and by further

15   See Iamblichus, *De mysteriis* 3.25.

establishing them. First, it grants that the same things can be treated from two different perspectives without one of them cancelling the other; thus there can be two different sciences of God. Second, it provides the basis for the two sciences: one functions through the light of natural reason, the other through the light of divine revelation. Moreover, they can, at least to some extent, keep out of each other's way because they differ "according to genus." Sacred doctrine is a fundamentally different kind of thing from the theology which is part of philosophy.

From the Divine Names of Dionysius to the *Summa Theologiae*

At least four ideas Thomas attributes to Dionysius the Areopagite occupy important places in the opening question of the *Summa theologiae*: saving doctrine depends on a descent of illumination from God, given to us in

Sacred Scripture; there it appears in metaphors; humans must begin from these sensible images, and indeed from the sensible generally; for theology, our lifting up of ourselves toward God is essential. Their appearance and importance are not accidental. Aquinas was working on his *Exposition of the Divine Names* of Dionysius at the same time he was writing the First Part of the *Summa*.

While expositing the *Divine Names*, Thomas used William of Moerbeke's translation of Aristotle's *Categories* (finished in March 1266), which went with his translation of the commentary of Simplicius on the same. The *Exposition* is the first of the long list of commentaries on non-scriptural books that Aquinas undertook in the wake of William of Moerbeke's new translations. Scholars frequently note the dependence of Aquinas's *Exposition of the "De anima"* on Moerbeke's translation of Themistius's annotated paraphrase of the same work finished on November 22, 1267, and the temporal coincidence between Aquinas on the *De anima* and his treatise on human nature in the *Summa theologiae*. However, the sequence whereby Moerbeke's translation of Simplicius precedes Aquinas's *Exposition of the Divine Names*, and the overlap in time and place of Aquinas's familiarity with the translations with the beginning of the First Part of the *Summa*, are less noticed.

Yet one of their effects may be a profoundly important change not only in Thomas's theology but in that of the Latin West generally. We have seen above that, by the time he wrote his *Exposition of the Divine Names*, Aquinas understood Dionysius to be using a Platonic "way of speaking" and Thomas judged this to be appropriate in respect to the First and consonant with Christian faith. Within that *Exposition* he set out the ways "one" functions as principle. We have also seen that he learned from Simplicius *On the Categories* that the Platonists characteristically "proceeded from intelligible reasons." When these are put together with the structure Aquinas discerns in Dionysius's treatment of the *Divine Names*, we have a basis for Thomas's own beginning of theology with God, for his separation of the treatise on God as one (qu. 3–26) from that on God as three (qu. 27–43) within his treatment of God

In the *Summa theologiae*, and for his placing the *de Deo uno* first there.

Thomas is said to be the originator of this fundamental structural determinant of the treatise on God, and that it appears for the first time in his *Summa theologiae*. While it has been maintained that either Augustinian or Aristotelian rationalism (or both!) underlies his division and ordering of the treatise, Thomas is explicit that he finds this distinction, and the reason for beginning from the divine as one and good, in Dionysius, and that no reduction of theology to philosophical reason is involved. Dionysius said that he separated the consideration of the undifferentiated and the differentiated names into distinct treatises.[16] Thomas hears from Dionysius that "one has the nature of the principle."[17] Further, clearly using the *Divine Names* as a model, he begins his own treatise on God with one under the form of simplicity, from which perfection and goodness immediately follow.

16 See Aquinas, *In De divinis nominibus* I.i, §§ 1–3; II, i, § 110, §121, §§126–7; II, ii, §141.
17 Ibid., II, ii, §143. See also, II, ii, §135.

By a Neoplatonic logic, having begun the treatise with simplicity, Aquinas concludes its first section with God's unity. Moreover, in the *Divine Names*, he also finds the logic by which he will treat the procession of creatures after the procession of the divine persons, because they all act together in creation.[18]

18   See ibid., II, ii, §153.

CHAPTER FOUR
From Impassibility to Self-Affectivity: The Trinitarian Metaphysics of Esse in Thomas's *Summa Theologiae*

The Moving Circles of Theology

Così vid' ïo la gloriosa rota muoversi.[1]

1   Dante, *Paradiso* 10.145: "So I saw the glorious wheel move."

In Thomas's rightly ordered *Summa theologiae*,[2] sacred doctrine exercises its privilege to begin treating its subject, God, with himself. Although "faith presupposes natural knowledge, as grace does nature," when Aquinas sets out as preamble to demonstrate the existence of God because it is the first necessity of our theology,[3] we hear: "'I am Who am' said by the person of God."[4] Thus coordinately and simultaneously, though differing in kind from revealed theology, philosophical theology rises from God's effects so as to make the divine speech intelligible to us. We are led to what is above reason by developing our natural reasoning until we reach the philosophical sciences and certain conceptual knowing.[5] Elsewhere, when drawing the circles described by these rising and descending movements, Aquinas takes us back to the origins when he,

2 See *ST*, prologue.
3 See *ST* I, qu. 2, art. 2, ad 1; cf. *De veritate*, qu. 10, art. 12.
4 *ST* I, qu. 2, art. 3: "Sed contra est quod dicitur Exodi III, ex persona Dei, *ego sum qui sum.*"
5 See *ST* I, qu. 1, art. 1, ad 2 and I, qu. 1, art. 5, ad 2.

unknowingly, quotes Heraclitus: "the way up
and the way down are the same."[6] My aim is
to set out the encirclings by which Thomas's
multilayered thearchy manifests the God who
includes and embraces us within a cosmos
material and spiritual. However, before enter-
ing those perfect, or motionless, motions, let
us consider, besides the one way by which philosophy ascends and God's self-knowledge de-
scends, the other great circle described by all
things, the circle of conversion.

Conversion, as the structure of all except
the First, was worked out most completely
and scientifically by Proclus. For Proclus, all
reality beneath the One–Good is structured by
monē–proodos–epistrophē; all is in the First,
proceeds from it, and is converted back towards it when it achieves its proper good.[7]
Aquinas's most weighty authorities for the

6   Aquinas, *Summa contra gentiles* 4.1.3: "eadem
    est via qua descenditur et ascenditur," which
    quotes Heraclitus: "ὁδὸς ἄνω κάτω μία καὶ ὡυτή"
    (Diels, B60).
7   See Aquinas, *In De divinis nominibus*, XIII, xiii,
    §986: "ad Deum convertuntur omnia, sicut ad
    finem et adimplentur, idest perficiuntur omnia:

Proclean formation are Dionysius and the *Liber de causis*. Augustine's Trinitarian theology enables importing this conversion into God himself. It structures Aquinas's whole theological cosmic system and its parts.

The logic of Aquinas's treatment of God in himself is manifested first in the five ways to the existence of God, and its basic structure does not vary until its completion in the sending of the divine persons. There what has come to be called "mystical experience" enters with the language of touching, common to the tradition from Plato and Aristotle and, crucially for Aquinas, to Plotinus[8] and Augustine.[9] By grace, the soul, in this life, "touches (*attingit*) God himself":

> God is in all things by his essence, power, and presence, according to

ultima enim rei perfectio est ex eo quod attingit proprium finem."

8   See Plotinus, *Ennead* 6.9.4. It is remarkable how much of the Plotinian doctrine comes down intact to Aquinas.

9   See Augustine, *Confessions* 9.10.25: "attingimus aeternam sapientiam"; 9.10.24: "attingimus eam modice toto ictu cordis."

his common mode, as the cause existing in the effects which participate in his goodness. Above and beyond this common mode, however, there is a special mode consonant with the nature of a rational being, in whom God is said to be present as the known in the knower, and the beloved in the lover. And because the rational creature by its knowing and loving touches God himself, according to this special mode God is said not only to exist in the rational creature, but also to dwell therein as in his own temple.[10]

This fundamental logic continues into the questions on creation, and thus into the *Summa* as a whole. Thomas's thearchy unrolls and rewinds by way of linked concentric circles ever more inclusive of otherness, until the *Summa theologiae* even encircles evil within the remaining–going-out–

10   *ST* I, qu. 43, art. 3, resp.

returning of the tripartite system of God, human, and Christ as the man-God. The divine Trinitarian life, as *conversio*, is established as containing both principle and end in the First Part. The return to God as Goodness per se takes place in the cosmos, fallen in the *exitus* of the Second Part—the cosmos which is the vast world constructed by humans because, as images of God, they are principles of their own works. That fall is a consequence of our pursuit of our good, happiness, and this quest contains the possibility of our return. Thus the Second Part is named by motion; it "concerns the rational motion of the human" (*de motu rationalis creaturae*). Each thing is moved by—indeed, is converted or turned back (*convertitur*) to—its own good, implicitly at least, the cause from which it proceeds, which is primarily and ultimately God.[11] The human motion is given a way back. By a Chalcedonian interpretation of the hypostatic union in line with the

11 Aquinas, *In De divinis nominibus*, III, ii, §94: "omnis effectus convertitur ad causam a qua procedit, ut Platonici dicunt."

humanism of the twelfth-century renaissance, the *Summa*'s consummation, the Third Part, "concerns Christ, who as a man, is the way of our tending into God" (*via est nobis tendendi in Deum*).

Order is on Thomas's mind when he begins the Five Ways, and he explains why we start where he does: the first, more certain, and more manifest way is from motion.[12] Aristotle's four causes are the deep background of the *viae*. Thomas uses them to structure his writing in the *Summa theologiae* at the beginning of the treatment of God when moving from creatures to God and at the end for moving from God to creatures.[13] Consequently, although millennia have flowed under the bridge between the causes and the ways, it is significant that in both places Aquinas employs the same order, one not used by Aristotle. Thomas positions matter and form between the moving and final causes. The source of motion is the obvious

---

12 See Aquinas, *De substantiis separatis*, cap. 2, p. 44, ll. 11–13. Compare *ST* I, qu. 2, art. 3.
13 See *ST* I, qu. 2, art. 3; and qu. 44.

beginning, just as its opposed cause, the final, is the appropriate end. Glossing Aristotle, who also mentions their opposition, he says, "motion begins from the efficient cause and ends at the final cause."[14]

On the way up in the *viae*, motion actualizes matter's contingent potentiality; it is raised to formal perfection as the good, or end, it lacks. Since motion is evident to our senses, starting with it is a concession to where our knowing starts. On the way down the Trinity is cause. God as the principle of all procession—that is, the Father—knows the form by which he acts in and as the Son and loves the Son, and himself as end, in the Spirit. So Thomas completes the circle by showing that God is cause in each of Aristotle's four senses. Thus understood, the order Thomas uses in the *viae*, in distinction from his sources

---

14 Aquinas, *Sententia libri Metaphysicorum* 1.4: "Quarta causa est finalis, quae opponitur causae efficienti secundum oppositionem principii et finis. Nam motus incipit a causa efficiente, et terminatur ad causam finalem. Et hoc est etiam cuius causa fit aliquid, et quae est bonum uniuscuiusque naturae."

in Aristotle, belongs to their character as proof.[15]

The first way is from the bare fact of motion to the Unmoved Mover. The second is from the existence of distinct things; these require a first maker. The third is from a fundamental difference between things: some are necessary, some only possible (contingent); in both theory and practice, the possible depend upon the necessary, and thus we come to what is necessary through itself and gives necessity to others. The fourth way is from a second fundamental difference in things: they can be graded, as greater and less, better and worse; all of these require a standard of comparison: the greatest, the best, the most beautiful, etc. The fifth way is from the end of motion: corporeal unknowing things always or mostly operate in a way which will bring them to the best; this requires an intelligence governing natural things to their end, an intelligence. That intelligence, Aquinas says, we

15 See Hankey, *God in Himself*, 141, and Barbellion, *Les "preuves" de l'existence de Dieu*, 224, 250, 252, and 309.

call God, as we do also the conclusions of the other four ways.

By means of these *viae* we have arrived at

1) an articulated and ordered cosmos: from mere motion, we came to things or substances; these were ordered first as necessary and possible and then as greater and less, better and worse; finally all were united into one teleological order of nature bringing it to the best.

2) a cognition which can know it: the mind which has passed along the Five Ways is a sensing, making, judging, and intelligently ordering knower.

3) considerable knowledge of God: the Unmoved Mover becomes a Maker who is necessary through himself; he causes and is the standard of the greatest and best, the Intelligence who orders the movements of nature to the good as their end. This interconnection of the physical, *psyche*, and divinity is as characteristic of ancient and medieval understanding as is the mutual relation of the knower and known.

The Scholarship and Thomas's Method

Intellectus non univoce invenitur in Deo et in nobis.[16]

The beginning of the *Summa theologiae* and its treatment of God give Aquinas's most innovative, characteristic, enigmatic, and influential doctrines about what sacred theology is and about the relations of nature and grace, philosophy and revelation, in it. The *De Deo* then works these doctrines out in the movement from God as One to God as Three, from God as Sent to God as Creator. In these articles, the Platonic and Peripatetic traditions—pagan, Christian, Islamic, and Jewish—meet; positions of Plato and Aristotle, Philo and Clement of Alexandria, Plotinus and Augustine, Proclus and Dionysius, Avicenna, Averroës, and Maimonides, as well as Thomas's contemporaries are directly

16 *ST* I, qu. 32, art. 1, ad 2: "Intellect is not found with the same meaning in God and in us."

discussed or are in the background of the argument. In consequence, there is scarcely a passage in the initial questions which is not surrounded by a mountain of scholarship and controversy, historical, philosophical, and theological. I have been engaged with some of this: John Milbank, Catherine Pickstock, Jean-Luc Marion, Alain de Libera, Michel Henry, Gilles Emery, Ruedi Imbach, François-Xavier Putallaz, Serge-Thomas Bonino, Richard Taylor, Mark D. Jordan, Jan Aertsen, and most recently Thierry-Dominique Humbrecht and Philipp Rosemann have demanded my admiration and critical attention, in succession to A. Hilary Armstrong, Pierre Aubenque, Louis Jacques Bataillon, John Beach, Maurice Blondel, Vivian Boland, Edward Booth, Leonard Boyle, Denis Bradley, Stanislas Breton, David Burrell, John D. Caputo, Marie-Dominque Chenu, W. Norris Clarke, James Collins, Emerich Coreth, Robert D. Crouse, Lawrence Dewan, Hyacinthe-François Dondaine, Austin Farrer, Cornelio Fabro, René-Antoine Gauthier, Louis-Bertrand Geiger, Stephen Gersh, Étienne Gilson, Martin Grabmann,

Pierre Hadot, Robert J. Henle, Édouard
Jeauneau, Mark F. Johnson, Fergus Kerr,
John F.X. Knasas, Klaus Kremer, George
Lindbeck, Bernard Lonergan, Henri de
Lubac, Joseph Maréchal, Armand Maurer,
Jacques Maritain, Eric Mascall, Gerald Mc-
Cool, John M. McDermott, Ian MacQuarrie,
Ralph McInerny, Leon Noël, T. C. O'Brien,
Joseph Owens, Fran O'Rourke, Anton Pegis,
Joseph Pieper, John M. Quinn, Karl Rahner,
Louis-Marie Régis, Pierre Rousselot, Henri-
Dominque Saffrey, Eileen C. Sweeney, Leo
Sweeney, Jean Trouillard, Fernand Van Steen-
berghen, Rudi A. te Velde, Édouard Wéber,
James A. Weisheipl, John F. Wippel, Émile
Zum Brunn. The long list is indicative, not
exhaustive, and yet they all belong to the
twentieth and twenty-first centuries. It
crosses oceans and bridges denominational
differences as well as those between secular
and ecclesiastical academies. Aquinas's philosophical theology remains a focus of study
and debate.

I can say nothing directly about most of
the names on the list and write about the
Summa as well. Nonetheless, it may be helpful

for me to locate what I take to be Aquinas's method in the *De Deo* relative to the positions represented by a few of these names.[17]

17 For my engagements with these figures of Thomistic scholarship and controversy, my most important publications are these: "Thomas Aquinas and the 19th-Century Religious Revival," *God in Himself: Aquinas' Doctrine of God as Expounded in the Summa Theologiae*, "Denys and Aquinas: Antimodern Cold and Postmodern Hot," "Dionysian Hierarchy in St. Thomas Aquinas: Tradition and Transformation," "From Metaphysics to History, from Exodus to Neoplatonism, from Scholasticism to Pluralism: the fate of Gilsonian Thomism in English-speaking North America," "Why Philosophy Abides for Aquinas," "Philosophy as Way of Life for Christians? Iamblichan and Porphyrian Reflections on Religion, Virtue, and Philosophy in Thomas Aquinas," "Self and Cosmos in Becoming Deiform: Neoplatonic Paradigms for Reform by Self-Knowledge from Augustine to Aquinas," "Philosophical Religion and the Neoplatonic Turn to the Subject," "Radical Orthodoxy's *Poiêsis*: Ideological Historiography and Anti-Modern Polemic," *One Hundred Years of Neoplatonism in France: A Brief Philosophical History*, "Aquinas at the Origins of Secular Humanism? Sources and innovation in *Summa Theologiae* 1.1.1."

The title of the current chapter declares that Aquinas's metaphysics of *esse* is Trinitarian and, indeed, my principal aim in this chapter is to exhibit how this is so. This may lead to the impression that I have forsaken my criticism of Milbank's Radical Orthodoxy, and what I take to be its collapse of reason into faith and human philosophical ratiocination into angelic intellectual intuition. The opposite is the case, because the key to Thomas's differentiations, and the movement through them, is that the argument is step by step. We end with God as three, but we begin with God as one, which for Aquinas has the nature of the beginning.[18] We end with the Trinitarian self-diremption of *esse* into three infinite subsistences, but our reasoning cannot begin there. We pass by way of the self-reflexivity of God as knowing, but we begin with the circle described by the names of the simple substance. We get to real substantial relations in

18 See Aquinas, *In De divinis nominibus*, XIII, iii, § 983: "Dionysius ostendit quod unum secundum propriam rationem est principium omnium."

God based on internal opposition by way of God's self-knowing and self-loving, but these activities are not themselves the Trinitarian persons. And although the middle term here is the self-affectivity of the divine giving and receiving of itself to itself, I do not follow Michel Henry into a complete identity of philosophy and Christianity.

Equally, to take up the other side of the current academic intramural games, my title "from impassibility to self-affectivity" may suggest that I have given way before the polemics of Marion and Humbrecht against Neoplatonism (and in the case of Humbrecht even against Dionysius, because he is the medium of Proclus). In fact, again, the opposite is the case. As I have indicated, Thomas's division of the treatise on God he finds in Dionysius at his most Proclean. The step-by-step movement from the simple to the divided is as fundamental to that Neoplatonism as are the divine names as primordial causes, self-constitution, knowing as the self-return of simple substance, and the emanations which produce the divine subsistences and finite being. Thomas's treatise on God is not to be reduced to Neoplatonism, but Proclus and Dionysius are our guides when we laboriously follow its steps. Boethius and Eriugena can help when we try to understand why he repeats the same content under different perspectives. The mutual interplay of form and content enables both the transition from one perspective to another and our acceptance of the change to that immutable content consequent on these transitions. While our theology cannot start with being as Trinitarian, step by step our reasoning about it and its representation to us are more conformed as the multiplicity within the simplicity is more manifest.[19]

19   See *ST* I, qu. 32, art. 1, ad 2: "Sed secundo modo se habet ratio quae inducitur ad manifestationem Trinitatis, quia scilicet, Trinitate posita, congruunt huiusmodi rationes; non tamen ita quod per has rationes sufficienter probetur Trinitas personarum."

CHAPTER FIVE

The Metaphysics
of Pure Being

Unum igitur est prius omni multitudine et principium eius.[1]

The Structure

In the wake of Philo and Clement of Alexandria, by the end of the *quinque viae*, we have moved through physics to cosmogony. A cosmos has come to birth in mind, a process

1   Aquinas, *In De Divinis Nominibus*, XIII, ii, §
    977: "One therefore is prior to all multitude and
    the principle of it." See Proclus, *Elements of
    Theology*, prop. 1.

which will continue after the manner of
Dionysius and Eriugena in the questions
leading from God's simplicity to his unity.[2]
Through physics and cosmogony we enter
theology proper. Aquinas tells us that this
theology concerns not how God is, but how
he is not. He begins it with the circle proceeding from divine simplicity to divine
unity.[3] It is negative theology that removes
from God every kind of composition, bringing us to what we may locate within the categories of contemporary scholarship as a
metaphysics of pure being. With that in view
we can sketch Thomas's argument in the *De
Deo*.

Within the joining of the way up and the
way down entailed by sacred doctrine's use
of philosophy ("the way up and the way
down are the same"), according to the right
order for learning this subject (*secundum or-
dinem disciplinae*), the *Summa theologiae* as

2 This is how both Eriugena and Aquinas understand Dionysius; see, for example, Aquinas, *In De
divinis nominibus*, XII, i, § 939.
3 See *ST* I 1, qu. 3, prooemium.

a whole and in its parts describes self-related circles of

1) remaining (*monē, in Deo continentur omnia*);
2) going-out (*proodos, exitus*);
3) return (*epistrophē, reditus, ad Deum convertuntur omnia*), by which all things come out from and circle back to their beginning, God.

Three parts of the *Summa theologiae* accomplish this:

1) God (*de Deo*);
2) the movement of the rational creature in, towards, and into God (*de motu rationalis creaturae in Deum*);
3) Christ the Way (*de Christo, qui secundum quod homo, via est nobis tendendi in Deum*) uniting the two and thus perfecting the human movement into its source.

Within these there is the tripartite structure of the *de Deo*:

1) qu. 2–26 concerning God as one (*De Deo uno*), treating the essence of God (*ad essentiam divinam*);

2) qu. 27–43 concerning God as three (*De Deo trino*), treating the distinction of persons (*ad distinctionem personarum*) (qu. 2–43 together constitute the treatment *de Deo in se*);

3) qu. 44–49 concerning God as creating (*De Deo creante*), treating the procession, or emanation, of creatures from God (*ad processum creaturarum*).

The *De Deo uno* is again tripartite:

1) qu. 2: whether God is (*an sit Deus*);
2) qu. 3–13: how God is or, better, is not (*quomodo sit, vel potius quomodo non sit*);
3) qu. 14–26: the operations of the divine essence (*ad operationem ipsius*).

Whether the subject of this science, God, exists (*De Deo an sit*) is also tripartite:

1) art. 1: Is God's existence self-evident (*per se notum*)?

2) art. 2: Can God's existence be proven (*demonstrabile*)?
3) art. 3: Is there a God (*utrum Deus sit*)?

The Five Ways (*quinque viae*) have a circular structure, starting with the perception of motion (*sensu constat aliqua moveri in hoc mundo*) and concluding with motion's term in the final cause (*omnes res naturales ordinantur ad finem*).

From Motion to its End

1. What the *quinque viae* show

Ostensum est autem supra quod Deus est primum movens immobile. Unde manifestum est quod Deus non est corpus.[4]

In the *quinque viae* the Unmoved Mover becomes a maker who is necessary through

---

4   *ST* I, qu. 3, art. 1: "It has been shown above that God is the unmoved first mover, hence it is manifest that God is not a body."

himself. He causes and is the standard of the greatest and best; he is the intelligence who orders the movements of the unknowing natural bodies (*corpora naturalia*) to the best end. Aristotle's Unmoved Mover, "being in act and in no way in potential" (*esse in actu, et nullo modo in potentia*), is the incorporeal beginning of our knowing of "how God is or, better, is not" (qu. 3–13). These questions contain the conceptual names common to God's essence, as well as their circular structure from simplicity to infinity and back around to unity. The treatise, the names, and its structure derive, with modifications, from the *Divine Names* of Dionysius (and thence from Proclus). The first article of the treatise on God's simplicity (*de simplicitate*), which is devoted to the question of "whether God is a body," argues from what the Five Ways established. First, as the unmoved first mover (*primum movens immobile*), God is not a body. Second, more generally throughout the question, it argues from the necessity that the first being, as perfectly actual being, cannot in any way be potential, to the absence of composition in each and every variety. And so, by way of Aristotle's

causes, his Unmoved Mover, and his fundamental philosophical framework, we arrive at
what we can only identify as a Neoplatonic circle of remaining–going-out–returning.

The *De Deo* starts, then, with the impassible God of our title, "from impassibility to
self-affectivity." This God is set absolutely
against everything else: it moves, he is unmoved and unmovable; its potentiality makes
it movable, he is *nullo modo in potentia*; it is
composite, he is utterly simple, so simple that
he is *non solum sua essentia ... sed etiam suum
esse*, and these are identical in him.[5] Aquinas's
God begins as impassibly transcendent.

2. The circle described by the names of the divine essence

Question 3 (*De simplicitate*) shows that as simple, God is the *monē*, that in which all things
remain. *Esse* negates all composition, is
through itself form (*per se forma*) and thus
subsistent, and identical with *essentia*. The en-
trance to thinking the divine is the

5   *ST* I, qu. 3, art. 4.

Platonic/Aristotelian denial of corporeality to God. Question 4 (*De perfectione*), on God's perfection, continues the remaining: "God, in one existence, contains all things in advance of their emergence from him (*in una existentia omnia praehabet*)."[6] Perfection is a negation by eminence. God is not in a genus. He is uniquely the very being subsisting through itself (*ipsum esse per se subsistens*) and can have no proper likeness. Because God is absolutely singular—that is, uniquely as he is—creation can only be participation (a partial manifestation). Question 5 (*De bono in communi*) begins the *exitus*. Following Plato merged with Aristotle in the Neoplatonic manner, the Good for Aquinas is simultaneously efficient and final cause; as the end, it presupposes the other causes.[7] The Good is by nature self-diffusive.[8] In question 6

6   *ST* I, qu. 4, art. 2, sed contra; see Aquinas, *In De divinis nominibus*, XIII, i, § 967.
7   See *ST* I, qu. 5, art. 4: "id quod est primum in causando, ultimum est in causato." See Aquinas, *In De divinis nominibus*, I, iii, § 94.
8   See *ST* I, qu. 5, art. 4, ad 2: "bonum dicitur diffusivum sui esse, eo modo quo finis dicitur movere."

(*De bonitate Dei*), this is applied to God: "All perfections flow from him (*omnes perfectiones ... effluunt ab eo*)."[9] Thus the fourth, the most Platonic of the Five Ways, reappears.

Aquinas introduces the furthest reaches of the *exitus*: "After the divine perfection comes the consideration of his infinity and existence in things, for it belongs to God to be everywhere and in all things insofar as he is uncontainable (*incircumscriptibilis*) and infinite."[10] In question 7, concerning God's infinity (*De infinitate Dei*), we learn that "being itself is of all things formal to the highest extent (*maxime formale omnium est ipsum esse*)." Thus, it is infinite and perfect. Being form through itself (*per se forma*), there is no limitation of matter to impede it.[11] Question 8, on God's existence in things (*existentia Dei in rebus*), establishes that God exists in all things "intimately" (*intime*) and "immediately" (*immediate*), "just as an acting thing is present to that in which it acts (*sicut agens adest ei in*

---

9   *ST* I, qu. 6, art. 2.
10   *ST,* 1.7, Prologue.
11   *ST,* 1.7.1.

quod agit)." God is everywhere because he
gives everything its being, power, and operation (*ut dans eis esse et virtutem et operationem*).[12] But operations within the one who
acts (*intra*) and those outside (*extra*) are distinguished. Picking up from the negation implicit in the distinction of the interior
operations of knowing and willing from the
exterior operations of power, question 9 (*De
immutabilitate Dei*) begins the *reditus* by way
of negation (the preeminent mode for Dionysius), that is, by denying mutability of what is
pure act (*purus actus*).[13] As time depends on
motion, mutability denied leads to eternity,
another negation (qu. 10, *De aeternitate Dei*).
Inclusive as "totally simultaneous" (*tota
simul*), eternity is "not other than God Himself" (*non est aliud quam ipse Deus*) and "the
proper measure of *esse* itself" (*aeternitas est
propria mensura ipsius esse*).[14] Question 11
investigates God's unity (*De unitate Dei*). Because "one is convertible with being" (*unum*

12 *ST,* 1.8.1 & 1.8.2.
13 *ST,* 1.9.1.
14 *ST,* 1.10.2.

convertitur cum ente), every being is in some sense one; one adds nothing real. This unity is above things, because of God's simplicity (*ex eius simplicitate*); in things, because of the infinity of God's perfection (*ex infinitate eius perfectionis*); and of things, because from it comes the unity of the world (*ab unitate mundi*).[15] Thus, unity is an inclusive perfection, that is, unity contains the difference between the starting perfection, simplicity, and the many and varied beings which came out from it.

From the Circle of the Essential Names to the Divine Operations

Ipse est suum esse et intelligere.[16]

---

15 *ST,* 1.11.3; see Aquinas, *In de Divinis Nominibus*, I, ii, § 55, & XIII, ii, § 980: "Patet ergo ex praemissis, quod unum quinque modis habet rationem principii ...."

16 *ST* I, qu. 16, art. 5: "He is his own being and his own understanding."

The circle described by the move from simplicity through multiplicity back to unity is
only the first of many circles describing God's
inner and outer life. The next ones concern
how God circles upon himself in self-knowing
and self-loving. They come after two questions: qu. 12, on how God is known by us,
and qu. 13, on how God is named by us.

Then follow God's internal operations,
knowing and loving:

1) God's knowledge, ideas, truth, falsity, and
   life are treated in qu. 14–18. Qu. 18, devoted to God's life, is where Aquinas explicitly applies motionless motion to God.
2) God's will, love, justice, and mercy form
   the subject matter of qu. 19–21.
3) God's providence and predestination (that
   is to say, the combination of knowledge
   and will) are examined in qu. 22–24.

Next (in qu. 25) comes the *operatio ad extra,*
God's power. This is followed, after a summary
and transition, by God's happiness (qu. 26).

Beginning with the processions within
God and the origin of the persons in God (qu.

27), we come to the Trinity, personal emanations within God based on his internal operations of knowing and loving. Scriptural revelation is necessary to know that there is real relation with the opposition of giving and receiving in the essence. Then, starting with qu. 44 on the First Cause of all beings, we arrive at the procession based on power, which is outside God's essence, the emanation of creation. Here what receives is unequal to what gives (the divine essence united in the real subsistences), and the relation is not mutual but rather of creature to creator. In fact, that unequal relation of dependence is what constitutes the creature as creature.

1. How God is known by us, and how God is named by us

Ipsa essentia Dei fit forma intelligibilis intellectus.[17]

---

17   *ST* I, qu. 12, art. 5: "The very essence of God is the intelligible form of the intellect." Also see I, qu. 12, art. 2, ad 3.

In these questions we find three of Aquinas's most characteristic doctrines, ones determinative of his system: created grace, his astonishingly kataphatic version of how we name God, and his analogy of being. These are sharply opposed to the thinking of the figure who provided the authority, the structure, and much of the doctrine of the circle from simplicity to unity. In our progress from and in the divine unity to levels ever more inclusive of multiplicity and difference, we step out of Dionysius's circle into the differentiation of self-reflexive knowing. In Thomas's balanced system, with the questions on how God is known and named by us, and on the divine operations, dominated by knowing, Aristotle re-emerges vis-à-vis the Neoplatonists.

We arrive at God's knowledge from one of its effects, our knowing and naming of the essence in its going out from the perfect simplicity of *esse* to its multiplication in things, and back to its inclusive and exclusive unity. The likeness of our created knowledge to the divine knowing is by analogy: "according to a certain analogy, even as being itself is common to all things."[18] These questions sum up the first naming but do not themselves predicate a name. They are, therefore, a break in the argument, the second of several strongly marked breaks in the *De Deo*. Characteristically, the greater transitions are preceded by a gathering (here the name, unity, followed by a reflection on knowing and naming). As manifesting a created likeness, knowing and naming, in common with the *quinque viae* and Thomas's method throughout, are a higher step in the ascent from effect to cause. As self-reflexive, they move us further in the descent into the divine self-differentiation.

2. The operations of the essence

Dicitur in libro de causis, quod sciens essentiam suam, redit ad essentiam suam.[19]

18 *ST* I, qu. 4, art. 3: "secundum aliqualem analogiam, sicut ipsum esse est commune omnibus."
19 *ST*, 1.14.2 ad 1: "It is said in the *Liber de Causis* that what knows its essence returns to its own essence."

Listing all the Aristotelian conceptions function-
ing in the questions on the divine operations
would lead us astray, but some outstandingly
important ones are the following:

1) Knowing is an activity, *energeia*, or operation.
2) Knowing is a perfect or internal activity
   in which the object is in the agent.
3) Knowing is known in reflection upon the
   unity of knower and known.
4) A simple substance has perfect self-return
   and thus knows. (This is from Proclus,
   but attributed to Aristotle, by way of the
   Liber de causis; it is the philosophical
   basis for moving from qu. 11 to qu. 14.)
5) Naming follows on knowing.
6) Will, or desire, follows on knowing.
7) Truth is in the intellect dividing and uniting.
8) There is a productive operation whose object is outside the agent.
9) Knowing as self-complete is beatitude,
   and the perfect life of motionless motion
   is activity endlessly complete.
10) Human knowing begins from effects.

In the operations of the essence, two are perfect and internal (namely, knowing and willing) whereas one is imperfect and external (namely, power). For the internal (and thus perfect) activities, the object of the act is within the action: the known is in the knower, the willed in the lover. For Aquinas only from these can the Trinitarian relations come.

Concerning knowledge, the ideas, truth, falsity, and life (De scientia, ideis, veritate, falsitate, et vita—qu. 14–18): Deduced from the perfect return of simple *esse* upon itself and understood in relation to human and angelic knowing, these questions (and the operations generally) are centered around knowing, and they derive from it their figure—motionless motion—with which they conclude as enabling the attribution of life to *ipsum esse subsistens*. Crucially, knowing has a limit; it is not ecstatic: God's knowledge implies a relation to creatures as they are in God,[20] but his will regards creatures as they are in themselves (*in seipsis*).[21]

20 See *ST* I, qu. 14, art. 15.
21 See *ST* I, qu. 14, art. 15, ad 1.

Concerning will, love, justice and mercy *(De voluntate, amore, iustitia et misericordia—qu. 19–21):* Knowledge is attributed to the *ipsum esse subsistens* because it is simple and returns on itself; so willing, which is the impulse for a greater unity of subject and object than what knowledge gives, follows. The impulse and the unity are two sides of the same: "the more complete the coming forth, the more perfect is the unity between the origin and the term of the procession."[22]

3. Widening and strengthening of internal difference

God is in all things as the agent is in its effects, "as one who gives them being and power and operation *(ut dans eis esse et virtutem et operationem).*"[23] Evidently, this structure requires a thearchy with an ever widening and strengthening of differentiation. While the moving circle described by the divine names from simplicity to unity may merely belong to our

22 *ST* I, qu. 27, art. 1, ad 2.
23 *ST* I, qu.8, art. 1.

}105{

knowing and naming (I do not think that this can be Thomas's ultimate position), the operations involve such a widening in several ways.

First, there is just the fact of their separate existence, requiring a distinction between the *esse* and the operations of the *esse*. Again, this may belong only to our way of knowing; however, following Dionysius (mediating Proclus), Aquinas thinks this division is characteristic of spiritual beings.

The second must require more. Both knowing and loving in the *esse* require self-relation. The self-relation of *esse* is self-knowledge, and the affirmation of known by the knower is the further identity given in the ecstatic impulse called love.

Third, knowing is multiplied in the ideas. These too might be only the divine essence from the perspective of the multiple creatures, but this is made impossible because (as the next point explicates) the divine is also truth.

Fourth, because truth is not in things but is in the judgment of intellect (which is an act of comparison for Aquinas), to be called truth, the divine intellect must circle around itself to compare what goes out from it to itself as truth.

Fifthly (and finally), unless, impossibly, all God knows exists necessarily in virtue of its being known, will must be added to knowledge for the coming forth of creatures.

4. The determining principles in respect to knowledge and will in the First

First, simple subsistent being is without composition and cannot be affected from outside; its determinations are from itself (*per se*)—it is essence as well as existence. In consequence, the argument of the *De Deo* shows *esse* as self-determining and self-affected. The same holds for knowing, which cannot be affected by what is outside it or below it. Second, according to the Aristotelian identity of knower and known, the form of what is known is the form of the mind of the knower. With the Peripatetics, these two principles together prevent God's knowledge of the world of material particulars. For Aquinas, should these principles prevail in this way, God could also not be their cause.

From the beginning of his writing, however, Aquinas knows and uses the Neoplatonic principle (with its logical basis in Porphyry at the latest) that a thing is received (or known) according to the mode of the receiver (or knower). This principle comes to him early both from Boethius and from the *Liber de causis*; thus, he does not think of it as Platonic rather than Aristotelian. This principle modifies the Aristotelian identity in such a way as to enable God's knowledge of creation and is fundamental to the analogy of being and the positive knowledge of God by us.

Nevertheless, two things prevent this third principle from being sufficient to solve all the problems. a) If the First Cause is only knowing, and causes by knowing, then all it knows will necessarily exist (Eriugena draws a conclusion like this). To prevent his kind of result, for Thomas the emanation of creatures requires will in addition. (Moses Maimonides, whose *Guide of the Perplexed* was well known to Aquinas, works out this problematic.) b) The basis of the effect must be discernible in the cause in order for it to be known as cause. Ultimately, this requires the internal self-differentiation of *ipsum esse subsistens* to which we are attending. Its concluding result is the giving and receiving that is the Trinity and, as Trinity, is the cause of creation. Therefore, the necessary and natural emanations of knowing and willing are the origin of the voluntary emanation which is creation.

5. The operations of the essence of intellect and will together (*ea quae respiciunt simul intellectum et voluntatem*)

Concerning providence, predestination, and the Book of Life (De providentia, praedistinatione, de libro vitae—qu. 22–24): There is a third general distinction within the operations, in particular those with respect to intellect and will together. In order to allow *ipsum esse subsistens* to have its proper effect, *entia*, as themselves participated forms of *esse*, and thus as substantial and proper images of the cause that are causing as well as caused, Aquinas must go back to a distinction between providence and fate, one as old at least as Plotinus, Iamblichus, Proclus, and Boethius. He does this by distinguishing between providence, which is in the cause, and governance or execution, which is in the governed and requires the substantial reality of second causes: "Providence is not in the things provided for (*provisis*) but is a reason (*ratio*) in the mind of the provider (*in intellectu provisoris*). However, the execution (*executio*) of providence, which is called 'governance' (*gubernatio*), is something active in the governor and something passive in the governed."[24] As secondary causes, all except the last effects are agents of government.

Because different states within the divine correspond to, and also consist in, states of the creature, they bring out a reality appearing with God's knowing. Aquinas must distinguish modes in it corresponding to modes of the creature; otherwise things would be necessary and eternal in accord with the mode of absolute subsistent *esse*. These modes are indicated by such distinctions as those between God's *scientia visionis* (of what is) and *scientia simplicis intelligentiae* (of what could be but never is) in knowing[25] and, most strikingly, between the love which creates irrational creatures, the *amor quasi concupiscentiae*, and the

24 *ST* I, qu. 23, art. 2.
25 See *ST* I, qu. 14, art. 9.

amor amicitiae creating rational creatures with whom God can enter into friendship.[26] That this requires a different form of creative knowledge and love points us to the importance of the invisible missions of the Trinity.

From the Self-Reflexivity of Knowing and Willing to Motionless Motion

Voluntas cuius obiectum principale est bonum quod est extra voluntatem, oportet quod sit mota ab alio.[27]

1. God as other to himself

Aquinas maintains that "the knowledge of God implies a relation to creatures as they

26 See *ST* I, qu. 20, art. 2, ad 3.
27 *ST* I, qu. 19, art. 1, ad 3 (adopting Gilby's reading): "When the principal object of the will is a good outside the will, it must be moved by another."

are in God,"[28] because of the formal identity
of knower and known. The composition this
introduces into God (although constantly
denied by Aquinas because of the difference
between the divine and the human modes of
being and knowing) is allowed because, as
he puts it, when discussing the divine ideas,
"the multiplication of the ideas is not caused
by things but by the divine intellect comparing its essence to things."[29] By such reflective
comparing, real differentiation is introduced
into God; it is not merely our way of looking
at God. Beyond this, will is the impulse for
a greater unity of subject and object than
what knowledge, with its duality, gives. Will
is related to things as they are "in themselves" (*in seipsis*).[30] With it, because God is
moved by himself as by an other, the question of motionless motion arises again: God
is not moved by another different from himself, but by himself as other: "This is the

28 *ST* I, qu. 14, art. 15.
29 *ST* I, qu. 15, art. 2, ad 3: "multiplicantur ideae
    non causantur a rebus sed ab intellectu divino
    comparante essentiam suam ad res."
30 *ST* I, qu. 19, art. 3, ad 6.

way Plato said the Prime Mover moved himself."[31]

2. Motionless motion: reconciling Plato and Aristotle

Iste motus est actus perfecti.[32]

For Aristotle, and for Aquinas following
him, physical motion is the act of something
which is imperfect. Evidently, the perfect
God cannot move in this way. In the *Summa
theologiae*, both when treating God's knowing and when treating his willing, Aquinas
follows those reconciling Plato's self-moved
creator and Aristotle's Unmoved Mover. This
enables him to predicate life of God and to
have him moved by his own goodness. According to Aquinas, in the *De anima*

---

31 *ST* I, qu. 19, art. 1, ad 3: "Cum voluntas Dei sit
    eius essentia, non movetur ab alio a se, sed a se
    tantum, eo modo loquendi quo intelligere et velle
    dicitur motus. Et secundum hoc Plato dixit quod
    primum movens movet seipsum."
32 Aquinas, *Sentencia libri De anima*, 3.12.2: "This
    motion is the act of the perfect."

Aristotle teaches that perceiving and thinking are motions in the general meaning of the word, rather than in its specifically physical meaning. In this way, motion can include the act of the perfect. The result is to dissolve the difference between a first being which moves itself (according to Plato) and a first being which is unmoved (according to Aristotle).[33] Aquinas found this interpretation of Aristotle and the notion of God's activity as motionless motion in Dionysius, in the Aristotelian, Neoplatonic and Arabic commentators on Aristotle, and in many other ancient sources. Aquinas supposed that Aristotle did not assert against Plato that knowing was different *from* motion, but that thinking was a different kind *of* motion. So Plato taught that "God moves himself but not in that way in which motion is the act of the imperfect."[34]

3. From motionless motion to the self-affectivity of real relations, persons, in God

33 See ibid.
34 *ST* I, qu. 18, art. 3, ad 1.

Licet motus non sit in divinis, est tamen ibi accipere.[35]

In love God is "translated out of himself into the beloved";[36] thus love overcomes the division of knower and known, expanding the divine self-differentiation to a greater level of otherness. "Because relation in God is real, it is necessary that opposition is really there."[37] "Although no motion is in the divine, however, there is receiving."[38] The real opposition in God is the divine *esse* as given and received: "It is true to say that whatever eminence the Father has, the Son has. ... For the Father and the Son have the same essence and dignity, but the Father has them in the form of giver and the Son in the form of receiver."[39] Real

35   *ST* I, qu. 42, art. 1, ad 3: "Although motion does not exist in divinity, there is nonetheless receiving."
36   *ST* I, qu. 20, art. 2, ad 1: "amans sic fit extra se in amatum translatus, inquantum vult amato bonum, et operatur per suam providentiam, sicut et sibi."
37   *ST* I, qu. 28, art. 3.
38   *ST* I, qu. 42, art. 1, ad 3.
39   *ST* I, qu. 42, art. 4, ad 2.

opposition as self-differentiation in God is God's self-affectivity (a term I owe to Michel Henry).

4. Concerning God's power and happiness: three breaks, a summation, and a transition

In qu. 25 and qu. 26 (*De potentia Dei* and *De beatitudine Dei*), we move from the internal, perfect activities or processions, which become the relations of equals in the Trinitarian essence, to the external operation of power. It originates in what has no prior in any sense (the "Father") and is modified in the divine intellect and will ("Word" and "Spirit") to produce the emanation of universal being as an unequal reception. This relation of the unequal recipient to the divine *esse* is creation. Thomas holds that we cannot deduce real relations within divinity, the real giving and receiving of the divine essence. In this sense, although the Trinitarian real relations are formed from the internal activities of the essence, and are both necessary and natural, we need Scriptural revelation to be certain that they exist. This lack does not stem from weakness in their logical necessity but from the deficiency of human knowing.[40]

This crucially important break comes along with an inclusive conclusion. We return to the beginning of the operations in knowing because happiness belongs only to knowing beings and because knowing is the origin of will and power.[41] Comparably to the conclusion of the circle of the essential names—unity—divine happiness knows and enjoys its going forth in will and power and the happiness of the rational creatures who participate it: "He possesses the continuous and most certain contemplation of himself and of all others."[42]

40 See *ST* I, qu. 32, art. 1, ad 2.
41 See *ST* I, qu. 25, art. 1, ad 4: "Scientia vel voluntas divina, secundum quod principium effectivum, habet rationem potentiae."
42 *ST* I, qu. 26, art. 4.

CHAPTER SIX

From Relations of Giving and Receiving in the Divine Essence to the Creature

The Trinitarian Processions of

Ipsum Esse Subsistens

Problems arise for knowing the Trinity. First there is the inadequacy of the kind of knowing that human reasoning is to the same activity in God. God's knowing is his being. Then there is the complexity stemming from the fact that the relations are both essential, based in the conceptual names (notions), and real, and therefore also subsistent individuals. In consequence, the structure of the treatise on God as three is complicated. It has two circles moving in opposite directions. However, the fundamental logic, which is our concern, is simple.

Although the Trinitarian relations stem from the operations of knowing and willing, they draw us back to the identity of God's essence with his existence. They are not distinguished from it by being its operations, but rather are the relations of the essence itself in which it is opposed within itself as giving and being received. Despite this return to the origin, the *ipsum esse subsistens*, they are the last internal stage in its fundamental logic. They are the last of the internal circular emanations ever more divided and ever more inclusive of the preceding difference.

Formally, they are *ipsum esse subsistens* completely given and received in its self-encircling as knowing and willing. Because the terms of the relation are opposed, they are subsistences in or of the essence.

Real Relation and Opposition in the Essence

*Cum igitur in Deo realiter sit relatio …
oportet quod realiter sit ibi oppositio.*[1]

That by which the procession of creatures is
distinguished from the procession forming the
Trinitarian real relations is identified in this
principle: "the more complete the coming
forth, the more perfect is the unity between
the origin and the term of the procession."[2]
What is implied can be pushed further: divine
esse is accepted (*acceptum*) "insofar as it has
esse divinum from another," in fact, from God
as other to himself.[3] Because the divine processions are in the identity of nature, the relations formed from the processions are real.[4]
They are "by the mode of self-relation to

1   *ST* I, qu. 28, art. 3: "Because relation in God is
    real, it is necessary that opposition is really
    there."
2   *ST* I, qu. 27, art. 1, ad 2.
3   *ST* I, qu. 27, art. 2, ad3.
4   See *ST* I, qu. 28, art. 1.

another"[5] and assimilated to the relation of identity.[6] Thus, "it is clear that in God relation and essence are not other in being but one and the same."[7] "By definition relation implies reference to another according to which the two things stand in relative opposition (*aliquid alteri opponitur relative*). Therefore, since in God there is real relation, so there must be real opposition."[8]

God modifies himself on the way to making others. The knowledge which belongs to the divine *esse* as subsisting and returning on itself is modified as producing or received. "The Son is God as generated, not as generating deity; hence he is someone understanding, not as producing a Word, but as a Word proceeding."[9] "The Father and the Son have the same essence and

---

5 *ST* I, qu. 28, art. 1, ad 1: "per modum ad aliud se habentis."
6 See *ST* I, qu. 28, art. 1, ad 2: "assimilat relationi identitatis."
7 *ST* I, qu. 28, art. 2: "in Deo non est aliud esse relationis et esse essentiae sed unum et idem."
8 *ST* I, qu. 28, art. 3.
9 *ST* I, qu. 34, art. 2, ad 4: "intelligens, non ut producens Verbum, sed ut Verbum procedens."

dignity, but in the Father it is in accordance with the relation of one giving, in the Son in accordance with the relation of one receiving."[10] The same order in divinity applies to Love. Love proceeds from a produced mental word because we love what we apprehend (Aquinas is a pure Aristotelian here). "Origin in God is signified both actively and passively."[11]

The Bond of the Ecstatic Spirit

Father and Son are opposed as well as united. The connection of the two (*connexio duorum*) is the Spirit who receives his being from both as love: "If you leave out the Spirit, it is not possible to understand the unity of connection (*unitas connexionis*) between the Father and the Son."[12] This is the language and doctrine

10 ST 1, qu. 42, art. 4, ad 2: "eadem enim est essentia et dignitas patris et filii, sed in patre est secundum relationem dantis, in filio secundum relationem accipientis."
11 *ST* I, qu. 40, art. 1: "Origo significatur in divinis active et passive."
12 *ST* I, qu. 39, art. 8.

of Augustine. Thus the whole Trinitarian process is a conversion, an *exitus* and *reditus*, the basis of that other going out and return, that is, creation.

The Spirit has two opposed aspects. On the one hand, it is *connexio, nexus, unitas*, because it is the bond of love overcoming the opposition of Father and Son, as giver and receiver. As *Spiritus*, which is the proper name of the third person as well as the nature of divinity as such, the return to Spirit is return to the unity from which personal difference arises. On the other hand, the Spirit is love as ecstatic. Love is "an action passing from the lover to the beloved."[13] The Spirit is thus gift. Love is the primal gift, since, as Aquinas quotes Aristotle, "a gift is a giving that can have no return."[14] The Spirit is the love by which all graces are given. So, by the Holy Spirit, the Trinity comes in mission to humans.

In sum, the divine Love is both the bond of unity and ecstatic. In the treatise on God

13 *ST* I, qu. 37, art. 1, obj. 2.
14 *ST* I, qu. 38, art. 2: "donum proprie est datio irreddibilis, secundum philosophum."

as three, the consideration of the Spirit is transitional. It is both the term of the outward movement and the beginning of the return to origin. These opposed aspects are the two aspects of the nature of spirit, "which seems to signify impulsion and motion." "It is the property of love that it moves and impels the will of the lover into the beloved."[15] So the motion and impulse of love carry both God *in se* and us back to unity.

With the gift of God himself by way of the grace of the Holy Spirit, we have arrived at the destination for which we set out:

> God is in all things ... according to his one common mode. ... Above and beyond this common mode, however, there is a special mode ... because, by knowing and loving, the rational creature by its operation touches God himself (*creatura*

15 *ST* I, qu. 36, art. 1: "Est autem proprium amoris, quod moveat et impellat voluntatem amantis in amatum."

rationalis sua operatione attingit ad ipsum Deum). According to this special mode, God is said not only to exist in the rational creature, but also to dwell therein as in his own temple. No other effect except sanctifying grace can explain how a divine person could exist in a new mode in the rational creature.[16]

From there only the emanation of the creature remains. It brings us back to the questions from God's simplicity to his unity because we have what is common to the divine *esse*, but now it is known to be acting according to its Trinitarian nature by knowledge and love. "God's creative power is common to the whole Trinity."[17] Indeed, when describing the character of creation as a real relation in the creature, Thomas takes us back to Dionysius's *Divine Names*: "The relation of

16 *ST* I, qu. 43, art. 3.
17 *ST* I, qu. 32, art. 1: "Virtus ... creativa Dei est communis toti Trinitati, unde pertinet ad unitatem essentiae."

the creature to God is a real relation, as I said above, and as *Divine Names* has it."[18]

Creation is the proper action of God alone, and its distinguishing characteristic is absolute being (*esse absolute*), that on which everything else in the creature depends, as effect: "That which is the proper effect of the creating God is that which all else presupposes, namely, absolute being."[19] Aquinas finds this logic in the *Liber de causis*. Creation is the emanation of the whole of being from the universal being (*emanatio totius esse ab ente universale*).[20] In consequence, when we arrive at creation, we must return to *esse*. Aquinas argues that "it is necessary that more universal effects be reduced to more universal and prior causes. Among all effects, the most universal is being itself (*ipsum esse*). Consequently, this is the proper effect of the first and most universal cause, namely, God."[21]

18 ST I, qu. 45, art. 3, ad 1: "Relatio vero creaturae ad Deum est relatio realis, ut supra dictum est, cum de divinis Nominibus ageretur."
19 *ST* I, qu. 45, art. 5.
20 *ST* I, qu. 45, art. 4, ad 1.
21 *ST* I, qu. 45, art. 5.

Because there is no motion or mutation in the act of creation, we remain within the logic of relation and of the opposition of giving and receiving. Creation involves diverse relations in the Creator and the created. It is the divine essence given and received: "Creation is passively accepted in the creature and is the creature."[22] Or, put another way, it is God as creature. However, although the relation of the creature to God is real, there is a crucial Neoplatonic inequality. The relation is not mutual; creation is a real relation of the creature to God, but not of God to the creature. And so, as in Plato's *Timaeus*, because there cannot be identity between the divine cause and the creature,[23] in order for the creature to be as much like the Creator as possible, difference must be introduced. "The perfection of the universe consists in the diversity of things. ... In consequence, the distinction of things and their multiplicity comes from the intention of the primary agent,

22 *ST* I, qu. 45, art. 3, ad 2: "Creatio passive accepta est in creatura, et est creatura."
23 See Plato, *Timaeus*, 37d4, 39e2, etc.

God."[24] He produces things in order to communicate and represent his goodness. No single creature is adequate to this; therefore, he produces a multitude of creatures of diverse kinds. The difference between the Creator and the creature, the motive of creation, and the means by which it is accomplished are Platonic through and through.

Conclusion: Thomas's Trinitarian Metaphysics of *Esse* and His Neoplatonism

As we have followed our teacher step by step from "'I am Who am' said by the person of God" to the mission of the Spirit, fundamentals of his understanding of being have been revealed. Because *esse* is self-affecting, God is Trinity. The Incarnation is not added at the end of the system; its deep ground begins showing itself from the beginning in the

24 *ST* I, qu. 47, art. 1.

Identity of God's existence with what he is. The divine generosity does not blind and sink us with its brilliance and immensity, but adapts itself to the modes of our reception.

Thomas tells us in the introductory question of the *Summa*:

> God provides for all things as is proper to the nature of each of them. It is natural that humans should come to intellectual realities by way of sensible ones, because our way of knowing has its beginning from sense. Hence it is proper that in the Sacred Scriptures spiritual realities are conveyed to us under metaphors from bodies. And this is what Dionysius says in the first chapter of his work *On the Celestial Hierarchies*: "It is impossible for the divine light to illuminate us unless it is surrounded by the covering of many sacred veils."[25]

25 *ST* I, qu. 1, art. 9.

In this passage we find the most authoritative source for, and a foundation of, Thomas's Neoplatonism. Like the sun, God ceaselessly sends forth his goodness, filling each thing with as much as it can contain and adapting his gift to the capacity of each. God is thus always manifest and hidden. For humans as knowers, this revealing hiddenness takes the form of adapting the spiritual things to bodily beings whose knowledge begins with sense. For conveying sacred realities, the sacramental world of sacred texts, signs, and deeds is necessary. This provides the principle for our knowing generally. We rise to knowledge not just from sensibles (*ab sensibilibus*), but through them (*per sensibilia*). Aquinas's Neoplatonism is thoroughly Aristotelian, Iamblichan, and Proclean as his philosophical thinking employs these modes of reasoning and a great many more. This is why he is not just a Neoplatonist or indeed solely within any other philosophical school.

Further and crucially, as I hope this essay on Thomas's Trinitarian metaphysics of *esse* has shown, his Neoplatonism is thoroughly Christian. Although Aristotle's ultimate substance as self-thinking thought may give essentials of divinity for Aquinas, it has become three hypostatic moments in a relation of total giving and receiving, something well beyond Aristotle. Equally, although this alternation of Aristotle happens by way of bringing the Neoplatonic triadic of remaining–going-out–return within the First, this is something neither Plotinus, Iamblichus, Proclus, nor any pagan, Jewish, or Islamic Neoplatonist does or would do. Here Aquinas is an Augustinian who has taken account of Proclus and Arabic Neoplatonists like Avicenna. Thomas's metaphysic of *esse* is Trinitarian, and thus his system is Christian from the top and all the way through. God converts upon himself and draws us into the circle of his endless life.

Bibliography

Works by St. Thomas Aquinas
Cited

De substantiis separatis, Sancti Thomae de Aquino Opera omnia iussu Leonis XIII P. M. edita 40D (Rome: ad Sanctae Sabinae, 1968).

In Aristotelis libros De caelo et mundo expositio, ed. R. M. Spiazzi (Turin/Rome: Marietti, 1952).

In duodecim libros Metaphysicorum Aristotelis expositio, ed. M. R. Cathala and R. M. Spiazzi (Turin/Rome: Marietti, 1964).

In librum Beati Dionysii De divinis nominibus expositio, ed. C. Pera (Turin/Rome: Marietti, 1950).

Bibliography

*In octo libros Physicorum Aristotelis exposi-
tio*, ed. P. M. Maggiolo (Turin/Rome: Marietti, 1965).

In quatuor libros Sententiarum, S. Thomae
Aquinatis Opera omnia, ed. R. Busa
(Stuttgart/Bad Cannstatt: Frommann-
Holzboog, 1980).

*Liber de veritate catholicae fidei contra er-
rores infidelium seu Summa contra gentiles*, 4 vols., ed. C. Pera (Turin/Rome:
Marietti, 1961).

Quaestio disputata de spiritualibus creaturis,
ed. J. Cos, Sancti Thomae de Aquino
Opera omnia iussu Leonis XIII P. M. edita
24.2 (Rome: Commissio leonina; Paris:
Éditions du Cerf, 2000).

Quaestiones disputatae de anima, ed. B.-C.
Bazán, Sancti Thomae de Aquino Opera
omnia iussu Leonis XIII P. M. edita 24.1
(Rome: Commissio leonina; Paris: Éditions du Cerf, 1996).

Quaestiones disputatae de malo, Sancti Thomae de Aquino Opera omnia iussu Leonis
XIII P. M. edita 23 (Rome: Commissio
leonina; Paris: Vrin, 1982).

Quaestiones disputatae de veritate, Sancti Thomae de Aquino Opera omnia iussu Leonis XIII P. M. edita 22, 6 vols. (Rome: ad Sanctae Sabinae/Editori di San Tommaso, 1970–1976).

Sentencia libri De anima, Sancti Thomae de Aquino Opera omnia iussu Leonis XIII P. M. edita 45.1 (Rome: Commissio leonina; Paris: Vrin, 1984).

Sentencia libri De sensu et sensate, Sancti Thomae de Aquino Opera omnia iussu Leonis XIII P. M. edita 45.2 (Rome: Commissio leonina; Paris: Vrin, 1985).

Sententia libri Ethicorum, Sancti Thomae de Aquino Opera omnia iussu Leonis XIII P. M. edita 47 (Rome: ad Sanctae Sabinae, 1969).

Summa theologiae (Ottawa: Commissio Piana, 1953).

Super Boetium De Trinitate, Sancti Thomae de Aquino Opera omnia iussu Leonis XIII P. M. edita 50 (Rome: Commissio leonina; Paris: Éditions du Cerf, 1992).

Super librum De causis expositio, ed. H.-D. Saffrey, 2nd ed. (Paris: Vrin, 2002). English translation: *Commentary on the Book of Causes*. Translated and annotated by Vincent A. Guagliardo, Charles R. Hess, Richard C. Taylor. Introduction by Vincent A. Guagliardo. Thomas Aquinas in Translation 1 (Washington, D.C.: The Catholic University of America Press, 1996).

Other Ancient and Medieval Sources

Plato, *Timaeus* and Aristotle, *De anima*, *Metaphysics*, *Physics*: references are all to the Oxford Classical Texts editions.

Augustine, *Confessiones*, ed. L. Verheijen, Corpus Christianorum, Series Latina 27 (Turnhout: Brepols, 1981).

Dante, *Paradise*, ed. and trans. Anthony Esolen (New York: Modern Library, 2004).

Iamblichus, *De mysteriis*, trans. with facing Greek text, introduction, and notes by Emma C. Clarke, John M. Dillon, and Jackson P. Hershall (Atlanta: Society of Biblical Literature, 2003).

Moses Maimonides, *Guide of the Perplexed*, trans. S. Pines (Chicago: University of Chicago Press, 1963).

Simplicius, *Commentaire sur les Catégories d'Aristote, traduction de Guillaume de Moerbeke*, ed. A. Pattin, 2 vols., Corpus Latinum commentariorum in Aristotelem Graecorum 5.1 and 5.2 (Louvain: Publications universitaires de Louvain/Paris: Béatrice-Nauwelaerts, 1971 [vol. 1]; Leiden: Brill, 1975 [vol. 2]).

———, *On Aristotle Categories 1–4*, trans. M. Chase (London: Bloomsbury, 2003).

Themistius, *Commentaire sur le Traité de l'âme d'Aristote, traduction de Guillaume de Moerbeke*, ed. G. Verbeke, Corpus Latinum Commentariorum in Aristotelem Graecorum 1 (Louvain: Publications universitaires; Paris: Béatrice-Nauwelaerts, 1957).

Secondary Literature

Aertsen, Jan, "Aquinas's Philosophy in its Historical Setting," in *The Cambridge*

Companion to Aquinas, ed. Norman
Kretzmann and Eleonore Stump (Cambridge: Cambridge University Press,
1993), 12–37.

Barbellion, Stéphanie-Marie, *Le "preuves" de
l'existence de Dieu. Pour une relecture des
cinq voies de saint Thomas d'Aquin*
(Paris: Cerf, 1999).

Chase, Michael, "The Medieval Posterity of
Simplicius' Commentary on the *Catego-
ries*: Thomas Aquinas and al-Farabi," in
*Medieval Commentaries on Aristotle's
"Categories,"* ed. Lloyd A. Newton (Lei-
den/Boston: Brill, 2008), 9–29.

Humbrecht, Thierry-Dominique, *Théologie
négative et noms divins chez saint Thomas d'Aquin* (Paris: Vrin, 2005).

———, *Trinité et création au prisme de la
voie négative chez saint Thomas d'Aquin*
(Paris: Parole et Silence, 2011).

de Libera, Alain, *Penser au moyen âge* (Paris:
Seuil, 1991).

I list my publications which will provide
scholarly substantiation for the argument of

this book. I have chosen the more synthetic so as to reduce their number.

"Thomas Aquinas and the 19th-Century Religious Revival," *Dionysius* 9 (1985): 85–127.

God in Himself: Aquinas' Doctrine of God as Expounded in the Summa Theologiae, Oxford Theological Monographs (Oxford: Oxford University Press, 1987). Reprinted 2000 in the series Oxford Scholarly Classics.

"Dionysian Hierarchy in St. Thomas Aquinas: Tradition and Transformation," in *Denys l'Aréopagite et sa postérité en Orient et en Occident. Actes du Colloque International Paris, 21–24 septembre 1994*, ed. Ysabel de Andia, Collection des Études Augustiniennes, Série Antiquité 151 (Paris: Institut d'Études Augustiniennes, 1997), 405–38.

"Denys and Aquinas: Antimodern Cold and Postmodern Hot," *Christian Origins: Theology, Rhetoric and Community*, ed. Lewis Ayres and Gareth Jones, Studies in

Bibliography

Christian Origins (London and New York: Routledge, 1998), 139–84.

"From Metaphysics to History, from Exodus to Neoplatonism, from Scholasticism to Pluralism: the fate of Gilsonian Thomism in English-speaking North America," *Dionysius* 16 (1998): 157–88.

"Between and Beyond Augustine and Descartes: More than a Source of the Self," *Augustinian Studies* 32:1 (2001): 65–88.

"Why Philosophy Abides for Aquinas," *The Heythrop Journal* 42:3 (2001): 329–48.

"Aquinas and the Platonists," in *The Platonic Tradition in the Middle Ages: A Doxographic Approach*, ed. Stephen Gersh and Maarten J. F. M. Hoenen, with the assistance of Pieter Th. van Wingerden (Berlin/New York: de Gruyter, 2002), 279–324.

"Thomas' Neoplatonic Histories: His following of Simplicius," *Dionysius* 20 (2002): 153–78.

"Philosophy as Way of Life for Christians? Iamblichan and Porphyrian Reflections on Religion, Virtue, and Philosophy in

Thomas Aquinas," *Laval théologique et philosophique* 59:2 [Le Néoplatonisme] (June 2003): 193–224.

"*Participatio divini luminis*. Aquinas' doctrine of the Agent Intellect: Our Capacity for Contemplation," *Dionysius* 22 (2004): 149–78.

"Philosophical Religion and the Neoplatonic Turn to the Subject," in *Deconstructing Radical Orthodoxy: Postmodern Theology, Rhetoric and Truth*, ed. Wayne J. Hankey and Douglas Hedley (Aldershot, England/Burlington, Vt.: Ashgate, 2005), 17–30.

"Self and Cosmos in Becoming Deiform: Neoplatonic Paradigms for Reform by Self-Knowledge from Augustine to Aquinas," in *Reforming the Church Before Modernity: Patterns, Problems and Approaches*, ed. Christopher M. Bellitto and Louis I. Hamilton (Aldershot, England/ Burlington, Vt.: Ashgate, 2005), 39–60.

"Radical Orthodoxy's *Poiêsis*: Ideological Historiography and Anti-Modern Polemic," *American Catholic Philosophical Quarterly* 80:1 (2006): 1–21.

Bibliography

One Hundred Years of Neoplatonism in France: A Brief Philosophical History, Studies in Philosophical Theology (Louvain: Peeters, 2006) [published in a single volume with *Levinas and the Greek Heritage*, by Jean-Marc Narbonne].

"*Ab uno simplici non est nisi unum*: The Place of Natural and Necessary Emanation in Aquinas' Doctrine of Creation," in *Divine Creation in Ancient, Medieval, and Early Modern Thought: Essays Presented to the Rev'd Dr Robert D. Crouse*, ed. Michael Treschow, Willemien Otten, and Walter Hannam, Studies in Intellectual History (Leiden: Brill, 2007), 309–33.

"Aquinas at the Origins of Secular Humanism? Sources and Innovation in *Summa Theologiae* 1.1.1," *Nova et Vetera* 5:1 (2007): 17–40.

"God's Care for Human Individuals: What Neoplatonism Gives to a Christian Doctrine of Providence," *Quaestiones Disputatae* 2, nos. 1 and 2 (Spring/Fall 2011): 4–36.

"Aquinas, Plato, and Neo-Platonism," *Oxford Handbook to Aquinas*, edited Brian

Davies & Eleonore Stump (Oxford: Oxford University Press, 2012), Chapter 4, 55–64.

"The Concord of Aristotle, Proclus, the *Liber de Causis* and Blessed Dionysius in Thomas Aquinas, Student of Albertus Magnus," *Dionysius* 34 (2016): 137–209.

"The Conversion of God in Aquinas's *Summa theologiae*: Being's Trinitarian and Incarnational Self Disclosure," *Dionysius* 35 (2017): 132–170.

"Placing the Human: Reason as Participation in Divine Intellect for Boethius and Aquinas," *Res philosophica* 93, no. 4 (October 2018): 583–615.